INA GARTEN
BAREFOOT CONTESSA
PARTIES!

INA GARTEN
BAREFOOT CONTESSA
PARTIES!

IDEAS AND RECIPES FOR EASY
PARTIES THAT ARE REALLY FUN

PHOTOGRAPHS BY JAMES MERRELL
FOOD STYLING BY RORI SPINELLI

CLARKSON POTTER/PUBLISHERS
NEW YORK

Published by Clarkson Potter/Publishers,
New York
Member of the Crown Publishing Group

Random House, Inc.
New York, Toronto, London, Sydney,
Auckland
www.randomhouse.com

CLARKSON N. POTTER is a trademark
and POTTER and colophon are registered
trademarks of Random House, Inc.

Printed in Japan

Library of Congress Cataloging-in-
Publication Data
Garten, Ina.
Barefoot Contessa Parties!: ideas and
recipes for easy parties that are really fun /
by Ina Garten; photographs by
James Merrell; food styling by Rori
Spinelli––1st ed.
1. Entertaining.   2. Cookery.   I. Barefoot
Contessa (Store)
II. Title.
TX731.G28 2001
642'.4—dc21   00-034698

ISBN 0-609-60644-1

20 19 18 17 16 15 14 13 12

FOR

FRANK NEWBOLD,

STEPHEN DRUCKER,

DEVON FREDERICKS,

AND ELI ZABAR,

WHO MAKE LIFE WORTH LIVING

Lots of extraordinary people helped me with this book. First of all, James Merrell, thank you for such beautiful photographs. Rori Spinelli again made the food look spectacular with seemingly no effort; and Miguel Flores-Vianna brought incredible style. Barbara Libath, who tested all the recipes with me, made the work so much fun. Parker Hodges and Amy Baiata, my partners at Barefoot Contessa, whom I admire and love working with, thank you for being so wonderful to me. Finally, a lot of people were generous with their ideas and recipes: Devon Fredericks and Eli Zabar of E.A.T., The Vinegar Factory, Eli's Manhattan, and Eli's Bread; Anna Pump of Loaves and Fishes; Sarah

Frank Newbold helps me make Butternut Squash and Apple Soup.

Chase of Que Sera Sarah; Johanne Killeen and George Germon of Al Forno; Michael Grimm and Jim Osborne at Bridgehampton Florist; plus my brilliant friend Ellen Burnie. • I owe so much to the Crown Publishing Group and Clarkson Potter/Publishers. My wonderful editor, Roy Finamore, helps me write the best (and most beautiful) books I can imagine, plus the invaluable support of Chip Gibson, Lauren Shakely, Marysarah Quinn, and Jane Treuhaft. • But most of all, I again want to thank two very important people: my dear friend Martha Stewart for being such a constant spirit and advocate for me, and my adorable husband, Jeffrey, who has believed in me always.

Barbara Libath and I make Rugelach together.

CONTENTS

Real Margaritas,
page 134.

AUTUMN

WINTER

Butternut Squash and
Apple Soup, page 221.

INTRODUCTION

I'VE ALWAYS WANTED TO GIVE GREAT PARTIES.

From the time I was married in 1968, I loved planning parties, cooking, and getting together with my friends. But in the beginning, I did some truly awful parties. As time went on I learned what worked and what didn't. I learned that small dinner parties were often more satisfying than big cocktail parties, that easy food meant I could spend more time with my friends and we *all* had more fun, and that the music at a party is sometimes more important than the food. But most of all, I learned to stay focused: Parties are "recess" for grown-ups, and I want everyone to go home saying: "Wasn't that *fun!*" So now I plan everything with that goal in mind.

By the mid-1970s Jeffrey and I were living and working in Washington, D.C. He was the deputy director of the policy planning staff for Secretaries of State Henry Kissinger and later Cyrus Vance. I was working in the White House Office of Management and Budget, writing the president's budget for nuclear energy programs. We were in our late twenties and far too serious. I wanted to have more fun, so I spent all my free time making parties for my friends. I would spend every evening after work cooking and baking, and almost every weekend we would have at least one party: often Saturday night, but I also loved to invite friends for Sunday lunch because the food was easier and it was a time when everyone was more relaxed.

Then one day in March 1978, I saw an advertisement in the *New York Times* for a specialty food store for sale in a town I'd never been to: Westhampton Beach, New York. I thought, if I love cooking in my spare time, why shouldn't I do it for a living? So my husband and I drove to Westhampton Beach the next day to look at a store called Barefoot Contessa. I fell in love. I DIDN'T KNOW ANYTHING ABOUT THE FOOD BUSINESS, BUT I KNEW THAT THIS WAS WHAT I WANTED TO DO. I made the owner a low offer for the business on the spot and we drove back to Washington. I figured, "We'll think about this, we'll negotiate, and then I'll decide if I *really* want to do it." The next day the owner called me at my office and said, "Thank you very much, I accept your offer." I thought, "Oh my God, what have I done?"

Six weeks after I'd bought Barefoot Contessa and I was still struggling to learn the business, a very good customer came in and said, "I want you to cater a dinner for forty people next Saturday night." I'd done my own parties for ten people, but professional catering for forty? I had no idea how to do it. But I heard myself saying, "Of *course*, I'd love to." I suggested poached salmon for dinner. She said, "Perfect!" and left the store. Poached salmon? I'd never made one in my life. So, I did the only sensible thing: I called my mother. She talked me through poaching a salmon in a roasting pan because I didn't even own a fish poacher.

The afternoon of the party, I took all the service people, the rentals, and the food to the client's house in time to cook dinner. Imagine my shock when I found that the oven was smaller than the salmon. So, I cut off the head and the tail, put the pieces in court bouillon, covered it with foil, and popped the pan in the oven. When the salmon was cooked, I reassembled the whole fish. The client fortunately never knew that there had been a

problem. (The lesson from catering: Be cool no matter *what's* happening in the kitchen.) I was on my way.

I have been catering parties professionally for more than twenty years now and, believe me, I've seen the good, the bad, and the ugly. Good parties take a bit of planning, but I think you'll find that they are *not* necessarily the ones that are the most complicated to produce. In fact, my experience has been just the opposite: I find that the best parties are often the ones that are the *easiest* to produce. With that secret weapon, I hope you'll use this book to discover new ways to have parties that will send all your friends home saying the magic words: "That was the best party I've been to in years." That's what this book is about: what we can do to ensure that we have parties that are not only fun for our friends but also fun for us.

STAY COOL

The most important thing about giving parties is to stay very, very cool. When I brought that huge salmon to my first catered party, I instinctively knew that the hostess must never, *ever* know that I had a problem. The same is true at home for your guests. They want to believe that you just whipped this party up in a few minutes before you got dressed, *not* that you've been slaving for a week and you're too exhausted to speak (which of course is how I *used* to feel before giving a party). Otherwise, they feel bad that you have worked so hard, and the party is off to a rocky start. How many times have we arrived at a party and the hostess is obsessing that the liquor store delivered the wine only fifteen minutes ago, or that the chickens in the oven are taking forever to cook? Don't *ever* let on that you're stressed. The thing to do is greet people at the door with "I'm so glad to see you!" It is, after all, why we invited them. These are our *friends;* no kitchen disas-

My desk by day is transformed into a dinner table by night (see page 24).

ter should overshadow that you invited them so you could spend time together.

Several years ago, my "cool" was really tested. One summer Sunday, I invited eight friends for lunch. A few days before, four people who were coming together called and said they had an emergency and couldn't come. No problem: I cut back my shopping list and decided to serve lunch in the kitchen.

An hour before the party, two of the people who had canceled earlier called and said they *could* come after all, was it all right? "Sure," I said, and sent my husband to Barefoot Contessa for some more rolls and lobster salad. Two other guests arrived— with three houseguests! Then another guest arrived at the door and said, "I have a friend in the car, can she come, too?" Now we were up to ten people.

I took a deep breath and made a silent plan. As soon as everyone was settling in with drinks, I slipped away to the kitchen, leaving the guests in the good company of my husband, Jeffrey. I moved the table settings from the kitchen to the larger dining room table, then I ransacked the refrigerator to find more things to serve. There wasn't enough lobster salad for the sandwiches, but I had chicken salad (fine for Jeffrey and me—who would know?). I divided the shortcakes in half and piled them high with extra fruit and whipped cream. Fifteen minutes later, we were all sitting in the dining room having a wonderful time, and no one *ever* knew what had happened—not even Jeffrey!

INVITING THE GUESTS

I have very few rules for myself, but one of them is not to accept an invitation from someone unless I *really* want to invite him or her back. It simplifies things so much. I don't meet the person in the street and feel guilty. We don't say, "Let's get together" and then *not* pick a date. Choose your guests wisely and you'll probably never have a boring party again.

When I'm inviting the guests, I think about a few things that will make a party fun. First, as I've said, I invite people I *really* want to see. Second, I like to mix interesting people from different worlds who might not see one another all the time. And third, I like surprises, what my friend Stephen Drucker calls the "flirt factor." It's fun to go to a party where there's someone exciting, someone who would be fun to flirt with. Years ago, I read a story about a friend of Paul Newman's who was having a really boring party; he just couldn't get things going. As the story goes, he called his friend Paul and asked if he could just stop by for a minute. The doorbell rang and there was Paul Newman in a yellow racing suit. He walked over to a woman on the sofa, kissed her passionately, then walked out the door. Everyone went crazy and the party turned out to be a great success! Sure, we don't all know Paul Newman, but I do try to invite a surprise guest whom everyone wants to meet. It creates a "buzz" and gets the energy of the party going.

HOW YOU INVITE PEOPLE SETS THE TONE OF THE PARTY LONG BEFORE YOUR GUESTS ARRIVE, SO BE SPECIFIC. "Come for cocktails from 5 to 7." "Join us for dinner at 7:30 to celebrate Phoebe's new book." "Skating and dinner at Wolman Rink from 6 to 9." A cocktail party usually has a defined span (5 to 7) and dinner is often open-ended (Come at 7:30). People want to plan their evenings, and the invitation tells the story. I also let people know how to dress by telling them where the party will be held: A beach party is very casual, a summer garden party encourages the women to wear summer hats and sandals; during the holidays

you might suggest "festive dress," which is "dressy" but not formal. I think it's important to let my friends know what to wear so they can feel comfortable when they come to my house.

PLANNING THE PARTY

I try to plan a menu with food that's fun to eat and in a place that's fun to be. Is veal with morels fun? I'm not sure, but grilled shrimp on skewers is! No one is particularly excited about eating a baked potato, but making potato pancakes together is a blast. I could never argue that it's especially fun to eat in the dining room, but a clambake at the beach with a big, roaring fire is always terrific. The same goes for Saturday night, when we all feel that we must get serious and do drinks and nibbles, appetizers, and a dinner with lots of courses. Help! I like to invite friends at other, easier times, such as breakfast on Sunday—which can be as simple as big pitchers of tropical smoothies, muffins that you mixed the night before, platters of fresh fruit, and big pots of coffee. Lunch can be bowls of soup, baked ham, a big green salad, and apple crisp for dessert. I also love to invite my friends to come and cook with me. Sometimes I'll make a big batch of dough and everyone can assemble their own pizza, or I make all the fillings for pita bread and everyone makes sandwiches (read on for recipes and menus).

Surprise your guests—have dinner in the study by the fireplace.

There are lots of parties to give besides the traditional dinner on Saturday night, and it takes only a little inventiveness to think of them. An offbeat menu, a few unexpected guests, an unusual location, great music—all of these get a party off to a great start.

I often read books on entertaining as inspiration for making my own parties. I hope each reader will personalize the ideas in this book for his or her own parties. The New Year's Day Lunch with three soups and a buffet for twenty can become an autumn lunch for eight with only one of the soups, and you can save the ham for another time. The Football Party with lots of sandwiches can become lobster rolls for six people that you take to the beach in August with brownies that you bought at a bakery. And I hope you'll take the recipes in the English Tea party—especially the carrot cake cupcakes—and make them for dessert anytime of the year.

I CAN'T SAY ENOUGH ABOUT ASSEMBLING FOOD rather than cooking. I keep telling myself that my friends won't have more fun if I spend two days making a daquoise for dessert than if I find a delicious pound cake at a bakery and serve it with store-bought lemon curd and fresh raspberries. In fact, they'll have *more* fun, because I'm relaxed and having fun, too. Keep your eye on the prize—it's *fun!* And I hope you'll find some ideas in this book that will have your friends admiring your ability to give parties that are *truly* fun.

Assembled desserts (clockwise): Pound cake, lemon curd, and raspberries; vin santo as accompaniment; fresh figs, honey, blue cheese, and walnuts; and a brownie with ice cream and chocolate sauce.

SPRING PARTIES

A Party for Eight

Roasted Asparagus with Scrambled Eggs

Sour Cream Coffee Cake

Tropical Smoothies

SUNDAY BREAKFAST

Eli's Health Bread

Raspberry Butter

Cinnamon Honey Butter

Fresh Fruit

Coffee

MY FIRST PARTY

I'll never forget the *worst* party I ever gave. It was 1969, my husband and I had just gotten married, and we were living in North Carolina. I decided to have a big Sunday brunch, and I wanted it to be fabulous. My first mistake was to invite twenty people I hardly knew. The second mistake was to spend a week getting ready, so I was exhausted before the first guest arrived. Worst of all, I decided to make a fresh omelet for each guest. Was I crazy?

As each person arrived, I had to run to the kitchen to fix a drink. Then everyone sat in a big circle in the living room while I spent what seemed to be hours at the stove making omelets, one at a time. There wasn't a sound from the living room—no talking, no laughter. But how could there be? I was the hostess but I was in the kitchen! It seemed like the longest day of my life, and I think it took me a year to build up the courage to give another party.

I knew immediately what I'd done wrong. A good party is *not* about the food, it's about the *people*. Now I invite friends I really want to see. I make sure the music is fun, to get things going. I plan a menu that is more about assembling food than cooking. And finally, I make sure everything is ready before my friends arrive so I can be a guest, too.

That fancy brunch has evolved into Sunday breakfast. I have hot coffee in thermoses out where people can help themselves. The table is set with baskets of fresh bread, sour cream coffee cake, and raspberry and honey butters, and there are big platters of fresh fruit. Scrambled eggs and asparagus are passed, and we're all together at the table. We have a fun, relaxed morning, and I'm happy to have the time to spend with people I love.

ROASTED ASPARAGUS WITH SCRAMBLED EGGS

SERVES 8

Scrambled eggs made with a dash of milk and some salt and pepper are a Sunday morning staple. Made with cream and Parmesan cheese, these eggs are a bit richer, and certainly fit for company.

2 pounds	fresh asparagus
	Good olive oil
1¼ teaspoons	kosher salt plus extra for sprinkling
	Freshly ground black pepper
½ cup	freshly grated Parmesan cheese
16	extra-large eggs
1¼ cups	half-and-half
4 tablespoons	unsalted butter (½ stick)

Preheat the oven to 400 degrees.

Break off the tough ends of the asparagus and, if they're thick, peel them. Place the asparagus on a baking sheet, drizzle with olive oil, then toss to coat the asparagus completely. Spread the asparagus in a single layer and sprinkle liberally with salt and pepper. Roast the asparagus for 15 to 20 minutes, until tender but still crisp. Sprinkle with the Parmesan cheese and return to the oven for 5 minutes, or until the cheese melts.

Cooking eggs over low heat ensures that they will be creamy and tender.

While the asparagus is roasting, whisk the eggs in a bowl with the half-and-half, salt, and pepper to taste. Melt 2 tablespoons of butter in a large skillet. Cook the eggs on the lowest heat, stirring constantly with a wooden spoon, to the desired doneness. Remove from the heat, add 2 more tablespoons of butter, and stir until it melts. Check for salt and pepper and serve with the roasted asparagus.

SOUR CREAM
COFFEE CAKE
SERVES 8 TO 10

This is the ultimate breakfast treat. My goal was a homemade version of a Drake's Cake, but better. As if the cake wasn't delicious enough, I decided to drizzle maple icing on the top and give it an extra-special flavor. This recipe can also be made into sour cream coffee cake muffins.

12 tablespoons	unsalted butter (1½ sticks) at room-temperature
1½ cups	granulated sugar
3	extra-large eggs at room temperature
1½ teaspoons	pure vanilla extract
1¼ cups	sour cream
2½ cups	cake flour (*not* self-rising)
2 teaspoons	baking powder
½ teaspoon	baking soda
½ teaspoon	kosher salt

FOR THE STREUSEL

¾ cup	light brown sugar, packed
½ cup	all-purpose flour
1½ teaspoons	ground cinnamon
¼ teaspoon	kosher salt
3 tablespoons	cold unsalted butter, cut into pieces
¾ cup	chopped walnuts (optional)

FOR THE GLAZE

½ cup	confectioners' sugar
2 tablespoons	real maple syrup

If you don't have cake flour, you can substitute 2¼ cups all-purpose flour plus ¼ cup cornstarch.

Preheat the oven to 350 degrees. Grease and flour a 10-inch tube pan.

(recipe continues on next page)

*If the eggs are cold,
place the whole
eggs in a bowl of
warm water for
5 minutes before
cracking them.*

Cream the butter and sugar in the bowl of an electric mixer fitted with the paddle attachment for 4 to 5 minutes, until light. Add the eggs one at a time, then add the vanilla and sour cream. In a separate bowl, sift together the flour, baking powder, baking soda, and salt. With the mixer on low, add the flour mixture to the batter until just combined. Finish stirring with a spatula to be sure the batter is completely mixed.

For the streusel, place the brown sugar, flour, cinnamon, salt, and butter in a bowl and pinch together with your fingers until it forms a crumble. Mix in the walnuts, if desired.

Spoon half the batter into the pan and spread it out with a knife. Sprinkle with ¾ cup streusel. Spoon the rest of the batter in the pan, spread it out, and scatter the remaining streusel on top. Bake for 50 to 60 minutes, until a cake tester comes out clean.

Let cool on a wire rack for at least 30 minutes. Carefully transfer the cake, streusel-side up, onto a serving plate. Whisk the confectioners' sugar and maple syrup together, adding a few drops of water if necessary, to make the glaze runny. Drizzle as much as you like over the cake with a fork or spoon.

TROPICAL
SMOOTHIES

SERVES 8

How nice is it when something that tastes so good is also good for you? I love to serve these smoothies instead of orange juice for Sunday breakfast. You can substitute raspberries for the mango and papaya to make banana raspberry smoothies. Yummmm. . . .

2	mangos, peeled, seeded and chopped (1½ cups)
2	papayas, peeled, seeded, and chopped (3 cups)
3	ripe bananas
¾ cup	freshly squeezed orange juice
1½ cups	skim milk
¾ cup	nonfat yogurt
1 tablespoon	good honey
6 cups	ice

Combine ½ cup mango, 1 cup papaya, 1 banana, ¼ cup orange juice, ½ cup milk, ¼ cup yogurt, 1 teaspoon honey, ½ cup water, and 2 cups ice in a blender and process until smooth. Make two more batches, or until all the ingredients are used. Serve.

When mangos and papayas are ripe, they smell ripe. The mango and papaya should also be soft to the touch and the banana a nice yellow with brown speckles.

RASPBERRY BUTTER

MAKES 1 CUP

¼ pound	unsalted butter at room temperature
½ cup	good raspberry preserves
⅛ teaspoon	kosher salt

Combine the butter, raspberry preserves, and salt in the bowl of an electric mixer fitted with the paddle attachment. Serve at room temperature.

CINNAMON HONEY BUTTER

MAKES ¾ CUP

¼ pound	unsalted butter at room temperature
3 tablespoons	good honey
¼ teaspoon	ground cinnamon
⅛ teaspoon	kosher salt

Combine the butter, honey, cinnamon, and salt in the bowl of an electric mixer fitted with the paddle attachment. Serve at room temperature.

Clover honey is from bees that visit only clover, lavender honey is from bees that visit only lavender flowers. Single-flower honeys are usually the best quality.

Eli's Health Bread can be shipped overnight from E.A.T. in New York City.

A Party for Six

Caesar Salad with Pancetta

PIZZA PARTY!

California Pizzas

Ice Cream Sodas

SURPRISE GUESTS

My friend Bob Currie loved parties. He was a wonderful interior designer and was often too busy to entertain on his own. So he and I would entertain together. I would do the cooking, he would arrange the setting, and we would each invite half the guests. I would invite my food friends and he would invite his designer friends. Surprisingly, they always seemed to have lots in common. Bob would invite an architect who I had been dying to meet, and I would invite a chef whose restaurant Bob loved. Once, Bob even invited someone who turned out to have gone to high school with me!

The challenge for a party where people don't know one another is getting them to connect quickly. This is when I love to have an interactive party—where the guests help make the meal. So it's the perfect time for a pizza party. Before everyone arrives, I mix a big batch of pizza dough (or you can buy some from your local pizzeria) and cut up all the toppings for the pizzas—peppers, fontina, turkey sausage, goat cheese, basil leaves, arugula—whatever you dream up. After drinks, we all go into the kitchen, assemble our favorite pizzas, and put them in the oven. We sit down for a Caesar salad with pancetta while the pizzas bake. The camaraderie of cooking together guarantees that everyone will get to know each other fast. But the dirty little secret here is that I don't even have to cook dinner; the guests do all the work. In fact, at this party, I also had all the fixings for ice cream sodas, and we all made our own desserts, too. How clever is that?

CAESAR SALAD
WITH PANCETTA
SERVES 6 TO 8

I adore a good Caesar salad, but most of them don't have enough flavor for me. This one packs a wallop. Making it involves a few steps, however, but everything can be prepared well in advance. Serve it alone for a first course before dinner, or add Grilled Lemon Chicken (see The Barefoot Contessa Cookbook) *or Grilled Herb Shrimp (page 138) for a hearty lunch.*

Pancetta is Italian bacon. You can find it in your Italian grocery or a specialty food store. Insist that it's cut ½-inch thick.

¾ pound	pancetta, sliced ½-inch thick
2 pints	cherry tomatoes
	Olive oil
	Salt and freshly ground pepper
2	large heads Romaine lettuce
1 cup	freshly grated Parmesan cheese

FOR THE DRESSING

1	extra-large egg yolk at room temperature (see note)
2 teaspoons	Dijon mustard
2	large garlic cloves, chopped
8 to 10	anchovy fillets (optional)
½ cup	freshly squeezed lemon juice (3 lemons)
2 teaspoons	kosher salt
½ teaspoon	freshly ground black pepper
1½ cups	good mild olive oil
½ cup	freshly grated Parmesan cheese

Preheat the oven to 400 degrees.

Cut the pancetta into ½-inch cubes and cook it in a skillet over medium-low heat for 10 to 15 minutes, until browned and crisp. Remove to paper towels and drain.

Place the tomatoes on a baking sheet and coat with olive oil. Sprinkle with salt and pepper. Roast for 15 to 20 minutes, until soft.

Wash the lettuce leaves carefully and spin-dry in a salad spinner. Stack the leaves on a cutting board and cut them crosswise into 1½-inch slices. Place them in a large mixing bowl.

For the dressing, place the egg yolk, mustard, garlic, anchovies, lemon juice, salt, and pepper into the bowl of a food processor fitted with a steel blade. Process until smooth. With the food processor running, slowly pour the olive oil through the feed tube (as though you were making mayonnaise) and process until thick. Add ½ cup grated Parmesan cheese and pulse 3 times.

If you're nervous about raw egg yolks, substitute 2 tablespoons mayonnaise.

Toss the lettuce with enough dressing to moisten well. Add 1 cup grated Parmesan and toss. Divide the lettuce among 6 to 8 plates and sprinkle with the pancetta and roasted tomatoes.

CALIFORNIA PIZZAS

MAKES 6 PIZZAS

When Alice Waters opened Chez Panisse in Berkeley, California, her use of fresh, local—often homegrown—ingredients revolutionized the American food world. When she opened the cafe upstairs at Chez Panisse to make what we now think of as California pizzas, she changed our idea that pizza was just a crust slathered with tomato sauce and chewy mozzarella. Make this dough ahead and let your friends assemble their own pizzas.

FOR THE DOUGH

1¼ cups	warm (100 to 110 degrees) water
2 packages	dry yeast
1 tablespoon	honey
3 tablespoons	good olive oil
4 cups	all-purpose flour, plus extra for kneading
2 teaspoons	kosher salt

FOR THE TOPPINGS (SELECT 8)

1	red onion, thinly sliced
1 pound	fresh mozzarella, grated
½ pound	Italian Fontina, grated
½ pound	mild goat cheese, such as Montrachet, sliced
1	red or yellow bell pepper, cored, seeded, and julienned
¼ pound	prosciutto, thinly sliced and julienned
1 bunch	arugula, cleaned and dried
6	plum tomatoes, sliced ¼ inch thick
4	pork or turkey sausages, cooked and sliced
1 bunch	basil leaves, cleaned and dried
4	garlic cloves, roasted
	Crushed red pepper flakes

FOR PREP

½ cup	good olive oil
	Cornmeal

(recipe continues on page 50)

Make sure the bowl is warm before you put the water and yeast in; the water must be warm for the yeast to develop.

The dough can easily be mixed and kneaded by hand.

Salt inhibits the yeast; add it last.

For the dough, combine the water, yeast, honey, and olive oil in the bowl of an electric mixer fitted with a dough hook. Add 3 cups flour, then the salt, and mix. While mixing, add 1 more cup of flour, or enough to make a soft dough. Knead the dough on low to medium speed for about 10 minutes until smooth, sprinkling it with flour if necessary to keep it from sticking to the bowl. When the dough is ready, turn it out onto a floured board and knead by hand a dozen times. It should be smooth and elastic. Place the dough in a well-oiled bowl and turn it several times to cover it lightly with oil. Cover the bowl with a kitchen towel. Allow the dough to rest at room temperature for 30 minutes.

Divide the dough into 6 equal parts and roll each one into a smooth ball. Place the balls on a baking sheet and cover them with a damp towel. Allow the dough to rest for 10 minutes. Use immediately, or refrigerate for up to 4 hours.

Preheat the oven to 500 degrees.

If you've chilled the dough, take it out of the refrigerator approximately 30 minutes ahead to let it come to room temperature. Roll and stretch each ball into a rough 8-inch circle and place them all on baking sheets sprinkled with cornmeal. (You will be able to fit 2 pizzas on each 18 × 13-inch baking sheet.)

Brush the dough with olive oil and add any toppings you wish, piling them high. Drizzle each pizza with 1 tablespoon of olive oil and bake for 15 minutes, until the crust is crisp and the toppings are cooked.

ICE CREAM SODAS

One year on the Fourth of July I decided that we had to grill hot dogs for lunch and have ice cream sodas for dessert. The best part was that Martha Stewart was a guest and she showed us how she makes great ice cream sodas. Have lots of different syrups and ice creams on hand so guests are guaranteed their favorite flavors.

Hershey's chocolate syrup
Strawberry Syrup (recipe follows)
Pure vanilla extract
Heavy cream, chilled
Club soda or seltzer, chilled
Vanilla ice cream
Strawberry ice cream
Chocolate ice cream
Coffee ice cream

THE EQUIPMENT
Ice cream soda glasses
Ice cream scoops
Straws

Pour 3 tablespoons syrup or 1 teaspoon vanilla plus 3 tablespoons cream in a tall ice cream soda glass. Whisk with a fork, then slowly, while still whisking, add the club soda until the glass is three-quarters full. Add 2 scoops of ice cream, add soda to the top of the glass, and serve with a spoon and a straw.

STRAWBERRY SYRUP

1 pint fresh strawberries, hulled and sliced
½ cup   sugar
        Juice of 1 lemon

Combine the strawberries, sugar, and lemon in a container. Cover and refrigerate overnight. Strain the syrup into a pitcher, pushing down on the berries to extract all the liquid.

A Party for Ten

Chopped Liver

Chicken Soup with Matzo Balls

JEWISH HOLIDAY

Brisket with Carrots and Onions

Noodle Kugel*

Perfect Poached Fruit

Rugelach*

* not kosher for Passover

SETTING THE TABLE

We've all been to boring weddings and dinner parties where there are huge round tables with enormous flowers, candles in the middle, and ten people sitting in a circle. It looks gorgeous, but you're stuck for the entire evening talking to the person to your left and the person to your right. I've spent lots of time as a caterer thinking about how to make this arrangement better.

In my experience, six to eight people are the maximum for a round table. For larger crowds, I like a narrow, rectangular table, and I put the most talkative people in the center facing each other. This way, the energy of the group is pulled to the middle and the party doesn't break into two groups (one group always has more fun). I also like a table that's a little too small so everyone is elbow to elbow; it feels more intimate this way.

When decorating the table, I make the centerpiece part of the meal. When I made this dinner, the challah was part of the table decoration, but another time I made the whole arrangement from the ingredients for dessert: clementines, dried apricots, and crystallized ginger. We can appreciate the centerpiece visually during dinner and enjoy eating it for dessert. I make sure that any flowers and candles are low in the middle of the table. In fact, I actually sit in a chair while I'm setting the table to make sure that guests can easily see over the decorations.

Finally, I love to serve family style. The menus for holiday parties aren't fancy; they include familiar foods from childhood that make us feel good. I put everything—the wine, the sparkling water, the platters of food—on the table so we can all help ourselves. Passing platters of brisket and noodle kugel gets the party going and makes this holiday feel like a truly shared experience.

CHOPPED LIVER
MAKES ABOUT 5 CUPS

Around the Jewish holidays, all our customers wait for us to make chopped liver. It's like your grandmother's, if you have a Jewish grandmother, but better. The Madeira adds a bit of sweetness without your knowing what it is. Be sure not to overprocess this spread; you want it chunky. I serve it with pieces of matzo.

2 pounds	chicken livers
1 cup	rendered chicken fat (see note)
2 cups	medium-diced yellow onion (2 onions)
⅓ cup	Madeira wine
4	extra-large eggs, hard-cooked, peeled, and chunked
¼ cup	minced fresh parsley
2 teaspoons	fresh thyme leaves
2 teaspoons	kosher salt
1 teaspoon	freshly ground black pepper
Pinch	cayenne pepper

To make rendered chicken fat, place the fat in a small covered pan over low heat until the fat melts. Store in the refrigerator.

Drain the livers and sauté them in 2 batches in 2 tablespoons of the chicken fat over medium-high heat, turning once, for about 5 minutes, or until just barely pink inside. Don't overcook the livers or they will be dry. Transfer them to a large bowl.

In the same pan, sauté the onions in 3 tablespoons of the chicken fat over medium-high heat for about 10 minutes, or until browned. Add the Madeira and deglaze the pan, scraping the sides, for about 15 seconds. Pour into the bowl with the livers.

Add the eggs, parsley, thyme, salt, black pepper, cayenne, and the remaining chicken fat to the bowl. Toss quickly to combine. Transfer half the mixture to the bowl of a food processor fitted with a steel blade. Pulse 6 to 8 times, until coarsely chopped. Repeat with the remaining mixture. Season to taste and chill. Serve on crackers or matzo.

CHICKEN SOUP

My husband loves it when the house smells like chicken soup. Nothing is easier or makes me feel better. This recipe makes a large amount; serve it for dinner and freeze the rest of the stock for another day. I make preparation particularly easy by washing, but not peeling, all the vegetables for the stock. This soup can be served with Matzo Balls, chopped vegetables, and shredded chicken.

3	5-pound roasting chickens
3	large yellow onions, unpeeled and quartered
6	carrots, unpeeled and halved
4 stalks	celery with leaves, cut into thirds
4	parsnips, unpeeled and cut in half (optional)
20 sprigs	fresh parsley
15 sprigs	fresh thyme
20 sprigs	fresh dill
1 head	garlic, unpeeled and cut in half crosswise
2 tablespoons	kosher salt
2 teaspoons	whole black peppercorns

TO SERVE

4 cups	¼-inch-diced carrots
4 cups	¼-inch-diced celery
¼ cup	minced fresh dill
¼ cup	minced fresh parsley
	Matzo Balls (recipe follows)

Place the chickens, onions, carrots, celery, parsnips, parsley, thyme, dill, garlic, and seasonings in a 16- to 20-quart stockpot. Add 7 quarts of water and bring to a boil. Simmer, uncovered, for 1 hour. Remove 2 of the chickens and allow to cool slightly. Remove the breast meat from both chickens and set aside. Return the remaining chicken and carcasses to the pot and continue simmering, uncovered, for 3 more hours. Strain the entire contents of the pot through

a colander and chill. Remove the surface fat, then reheat the stock as follows, or pack in containers and freeze.

To serve the soup, return the stock to the pot and reheat, adding the diced carrots, celery, dill, and parsley. Shred the reserved chicken breast meat into large pieces and add to the stock. Simmer over low heat for 5 minutes to cook the vegetables and reheat the chicken. Season to taste and serve as is, or ladle each serving over 2 warm Matzo Balls.

MATZO BALLS

MAKES 18 TO 20 MATZO BALLS

There are two keys to making matzo balls that aren't hockey pucks: Whip the egg whites, and use as little matzo meal as possible. Customers rave about our matzo balls during the Jewish holidays. Make them ahead of time and refrigerate them, covered with wet paper towels, in a little chicken stock. Heat them in the stock and serve one or two with each serving of chicken soup. I like rough dumplings, made by dropping them with two spoons.

4	extra-large eggs, separated
½ cup	good chicken stock
¼ cup	rendered chicken fat, melted
½ cup	minced fresh parsley
2 teaspoons	kosher salt, plus more for egg whites
1 cup	matzo meal

Whisk together the egg yolks, chicken stock, chicken fat, parsley, and salt. Stir in the matzo meal. In the bowl of an electric mixer with a whisk attachment, whip the egg whites with a pinch of salt until they are stiff. Whisk them into the matzo mixture until it is smooth. Refrigerate for at least 15 minutes, or until the mixture is thick.

Cold eggs are easier to separate, but room-temperature egg whites whip best.

Form balls the size of golf balls by shaping them with 2 spoons, rolling them with your hands, or scooping them with a small ice cream scoop. Drop them into simmering chicken stock and cook for 30 minutes, or until fully cooked and puffed, turning once. Remove and serve hot in chicken soup.

BRISKET
WITH CARROTS
AND ONIONS
SERVES 10 TO 12

Brisket is a great one-dish meal; the meat and vegetables are roasted together for hours. I make the meat ahead of time, slice it when it's cooled a bit, then reheat it with the vegetables in a pretty ovenproof serving dish. This recipe will definitely make enough to have leftovers.

6 to 7 pounds	beef brisket (see note)
2 tablespoons	kosher salt
2 teaspoons	freshly ground black pepper
1 tablespoon	minced garlic (4 cloves)
2 teaspoons	dried oregano leaves
1 pound	carrots, peeled and cut into 2-inch chunks
8 stalks	celery, cut into 2-inch chunks
6	yellow onions, peeled and sliced
6	fresh or dried bay leaves
2	28-ounce cans of tomato juice

I use Sacramento tomato juice.

Don't confuse corned beef brisket with plain brisket. Corned beef is the same cut, but it has been processed with salt and spices.

Preheat the oven to 350 degrees.

Place the brisket in a heavy roasting pan. In a small bowl, combine the salt, pepper, garlic, and oregano. Rub the mixture on the brisket. Pile the carrots, celery, onions, and bay leaves on the brisket and pour in enough tomato juice to come about three quarters of the way up the meat and vegetables. Cover the top of the pan with plastic wrap, then with aluminum foil. (The tomato juice will react unpleasantly with the aluminum foil if they touch.)

Bake for 3½ hours, or until the meat is tender. Remove the meat from the pan and keep it warm. Place the pan on 2 burners and boil the vegetables and sauce over medium heat for another 30 minutes, or until the sauce is thickened.

To serve, slice the meat across the grain. Serve with the vegetables.

NOODLE KUGEL
SERVES 10

I made this dish a dozen times before I got the right balance of savory and sweet, crisp and creamy. Now it's just right and not too sweet to be part of the main course. Naturally, children love a reason to have sweet noodles for dinner.

1 pound	wide egg noodles
5	extra-large eggs
4 cups	half-and-half
¼ cup	light brown sugar, packed
2 teaspoons	pure vanilla extract
½ teaspoon	ground cinnamon
1½ tablespoons	kosher salt
½ teaspoon	freshly ground black pepper
1 cup	ricotta cheese
1 cup	golden raisins

Preheat the oven to 350 degrees. Butter a 10 × 13 × 2¼-inch baking dish.

Drizzle some oil into a large pot of boiling salted water. Cook the noodles for 6 to 8 minutes, until tender. Drain.

In a large bowl, whisk together the eggs, half-and-half, brown sugar, vanilla, cinnamon, salt, and pepper. Stir in the ricotta and raisins. Add the drained noodles.

Pour the noodle mixture into the baking dish. Place the filled dish in a larger pan and pour in enough hot water to come halfway up the sides. Cover the entire assembly with aluminum foil. Bake for 45 minutes, then remove the foil and bake for another 45 minutes, or until the custard is just set.

I use Goodman's wide egg noodles—they're curly—but any curly noodle will work.

PERFECT
POACHED FRUIT
SERVES 10

Many poached fruit recipes call for Sauternes in the poaching liquid, but I was looking in my pantry and found the sweet Italian dessert wine called vin santo, which is traditionally served with biscotti. I thought it might be good instead of Sauternes, but I had no idea how good. Make this well in advance; it only gets better as it sits.

1	(750 ml) bottle vin santo
1½ cups	sugar
1	large cinnamon stick
6	whole cloves
1	vanilla bean
	Zest of 1 orange, julienned
	Zest of 1 lemon, julienned
10	whole ripe Bosc pears
1½ cups	large dried figs
1½ cups	large dried apricots
¾ cup	large dried pitted prunes

Vin santo can be very expensive, but there's no need to use the finest bottle for this dish. Any sweet wine, such as Sauternes, will also be delicious.

Bosc pears are the ones that are brown when they are ripe.

Place the vin santo, sugar, cinnamon, cloves, vanilla bean, and zests in a large, shallow saucepan with 2 cups of water. Bring to a boil, then reduce the heat to low and simmer for 10 minutes.

Peel the pears, leaving the stems intact, and scoop out the seeds from the bottom with an apple corer or melon baller. Lay half the pears on their sides in the poaching liquid and simmer for 20 minutes, carefully turning the pears once with a spoon. Remove with a slotted spoon. Poach the remaining pears in the same liquid. Snip off the hard stems from the figs with scissors. Add the figs, apricots, prunes, and the first batch of poached pears and simmer 5 to 10 more minutes, until the pears and the dried fruit are all tender.

Chill the pears, dried fruit, zests, and poaching liquid. Remove the cinnamon, cloves, and vanilla before serving if you like.

RUGELACH

There are lots of variations of rugelach, but this one, from baker Larry Hayden, is the best I've ever had. It's perfect for a Jewish holiday dinner, but we make them all year long and they're one of the most delicious cookies we sell. Make the whole recipe and freeze them unbaked. Then you can have a few freshly baked cookies anytime you want.

8 ounces	cream cheese at room temperature
½ pound	unsalted butter at room temperature
¼ cup	granulated sugar plus 9 tablespoons
¼ teaspoon	kosher salt
1 teaspoon	pure vanilla extract
2 cups	all-purpose flour
¼ cup	light brown sugar, packed
1½ teaspoons	ground cinnamon
¾ cup	raisins
1 cup	walnuts, finely chopped
½ cup	apricot preserves, puréed in a food processor
1	egg beaten with 1 tablespoon milk, for egg wash

Cream the cheese and butter in the bowl of an electric mixer fitted with the paddle attachment until light. Add ¼ cup granulated sugar, the salt, and vanilla. With the mixer on low speed, add the flour and mix until just combined. Dump the dough out onto a well-floured board and roll it into a ball. Cut the ball in quarters, wrap each piece in plastic, and refrigerate for 1 hour.

To make the filling, combine 6 tablespoons of granulated sugar, the brown sugar, ½ teaspoon cinnamon, the raisins, and walnuts.

On a well-floured board, roll each ball of dough into a 9-inch circle. Spread the dough with 2 tablespoons apricot preserves and sprinkle with ½ cup of the filling. Press the filling lightly into the dough. Cut the circle into 12 equal wedges—cutting the whole circle in quar-

(recipe continues on next page)

Rugelach is also delicious made with raspberry jam or just plain with the raisin and nut filling. These cookies freeze beautifully; defrost them completely before baking.

ters, then each quarter into thirds. Starting with the wide edge, roll up each wedge. Place the cookies, points tucked under, on a baking sheet lined with parchment paper. Chill for 30 minutes.

Preheat the oven to 350 degrees.

Brush each cookie with the egg wash. Combine 3 tablespoons granulated sugar and 1 teaspoon cinnamon and sprinkle on the cookies. Bake for 15 to 20 minutes, until lightly browned. Remove to a wire rack and let cool.

A Party for Eight

Raspberry Vodka

Rori's Potato Chips

Caviar Dip

ACADEMY AWARDS

Smoked Salmon with Mesclun

Filet of Beef with Gorgonzola Sauce

Roasted Cherry Tomatoes

Garlic Roasted Potatoes

Chocolate Ganache Cake

SURPRISE THEM!

How many times have you set out for a party and known exactly what it's going to be like? There will be the same crowd as the last party, you can almost guess what the hostess will make for dinner, and sitting in the dining room will be lovely but uninspiring. Entertaining for me is about recess, about time off from work and responsibility, and I think the best way to show people a good time is to surprise them.

Lots of things can be surprises at a party. It's fine to serve dinner in the dining room, but I'm always looking for new places to have parties. I've had several terrific dinner parties in my store in East Hampton; people feel as though they've been let into the candy shop after hours. I bring my best silver and china and set up a table near where the checkout line is by day. Another time, we all met for cocktails at the pavilion at the public beach, then came back to our house for dinner in the kitchen. In winter, dinner in the library feels warm and cozy; in summer, an evening picnic around a blazing fire at the beach is fun. An unusual place gives a party a spark that gets things off to a good start.

Another surprise that I like is to make exactly the opposite kind of food from what people expect. When the boss comes to dinner and people expect something fancy, I'll serve casual, hands-on food. When close friends come during the week, I've been known to go all out with the fanciest meal I can imagine. Just when people expect nothing special is when I love to serve caviar dip and roast filet of beef with Gorgonzola sauce.

For many years I've invited friends to watch the delightfully silly Academy Awards on TV. Everyone is expecting take-out pizza, and they're thrilled to be served an elegant meal. I think that's really fun.

RASPBERRY VODKA

Joanne Shumski's family owns a farm in Bridgehampton, and when raspberries are in season she makes raspberry vodka. Use this for elegant martinis, or make frosty highballs with Italian soft drinks such as lemon-flavored limonata or bitter-orange-flavored aranciata.

1 pint	fresh raspberries
1	(750 ml) bottle good vodka

Place the raspberries in a jar or bottle with a lid and add the vodka. Close the jar and allow it to sit at room temperature for at least a month, until the vodka is raspberry flavored. Store the vodka in the freezer so it's always ready to make icy cold martinis.

RORI'S
POTATO CHIPS
SERVES 8

When we were making the caviar dip for this book, Rori Spinelli, the food stylist, said that her baked potato chips would be delicious with the dip. Boy, were they! It was all we could do to stop eating them until the photograph was taken. And they're not even fried! How great is that?

	Good olive oil
4	baking potatoes
	Kosher salt
	Freshly ground black pepper

Preheat the oven to 325 degrees. Spread each of 2 baking sheets with 1 tablespoon of oil and put them in the oven to preheat for 10 minutes.

Slice the potatoes on the narrow side lengthwise on a mandoline so they are thin and flexible, about $\frac{1}{16}$ inch thick. Place slices on the hot sheet pans, making sure that they don't overlap at all. Sprinkle with salt and pepper.

Bake the chips for 10 minutes, rotate the pans in the oven, and bake for another 10 minutes. Flip each chip and then bake for another 5 to 6 minutes or until golden brown. Remove the chips to a paper towel to cool.

Repeat with the remaining potato slices.

To store the chips, cool completely and place in a plastic zipper-lock bag. They will stay crisp for several days.

CAVIAR DIP

This is a really popular dip at Barefoot Contessa, especially during the holidays. It's great on Rori's Potato Chips (page 77), but it's also delicious served with fresh vegetables or toasts. Use the best salmon caviar you can afford; we like the roe from Petrossian in New York City.

8 ounces	cream cheese at room temperature
½ cup	sour cream
2 teaspoons	freshly squeezed lemon juice
2 tablespoons	freshly minced dill, plus sprigs for garnish
1	scallion, minced (white and green parts)
1 tablespoon	milk, half-and-half, or cream
¼ teaspoon	kosher salt
	Freshly ground black pepper to taste
About 3¼ ounces	(100 grams) good salmon roe

In the bowl of an electric mixer fitted with the paddle attachment, cream the cream cheese until smooth. With the mixer on medium speed, add the sour cream, lemon juice, dill, scallion, milk, salt, and pepper. With a rubber spatula, fold in three quarters of the salmon roe. Spoon the dip into a bowl and garnish with the remaining salmon roe and sprigs of fresh dill.

Serve with chips, toasts, or crackers.

SMOKED SALMON WITH MESCLUN

SERVES 8

This is an easily assembled appetizer that's really special. There are many types of smoked salmon, but I prefer the drier ones, such as Norwegian and Scottish salmon, to the moister Atlantic or Pacific smoked salmon. Have your specialty food store slice the salmon paper-thin.

1	pound smoked salmon (about 16 large slices)
¼ cup	freshly squeezed lemon juice (2 lemons)
½ cup	good olive oil
½ teaspoon	kosher salt
¼ teaspoon	freshly ground black pepper
¾ pound	mesclun greens
	Snipped chives or lemon wedges, for garnish

Lay 2 slices of salmon side by side on each plate. Whisk together the lemon juice, olive oil, salt, and pepper. Toss the mesclun greens with enough of the vinaigrette to moisten. Place some greens on top of the salmon and finish with a garnish of chives or lemon wedges.

There is no substitute for freshly squeezed lemon juice.

FILET OF BEEF

SERVES 8 TO 10

I can't tell you how many filets of beef we've prepared for parties in East Hampton. It's an expensive main course, but it's very special and amazingly easy. This simple method comes from my friend Anna Pump, and everyone will think you've spent hours preparing dinner. This actually makes a lot for eight to ten people, so you'll probably have leftovers for sandwiches the next day. We serve the filet with Gorgonzola Sauce (page 84).

1	whole filet of beef (4 to 5 pounds), trimmed and tied
2 tablespoons	unsalted butter at room temperature
1 tablespoon	kosher salt
1 tablespoon	coarsely ground black pepper

The oven temperature is very important for this recipe. Use a thermometer to be sure your oven is close to 500 degrees.

Have the butcher prepare the filet trimmed and tied, so it will take you only a few minutes to get the filet ready for the oven.

Preheat the oven to 500 degrees.

Place the beef on a baking sheet and pat the outside dry with a paper towel. Spread the butter on with your hands. Sprinkle evenly with the salt and pepper. Roast in the oven for exactly 22 minutes for rare and 25 minutes for medium-rare.

Remove the beef from the oven, cover it tightly with aluminum foil, and allow it to rest at room temperature for 20 minutes. Remove the strings and slice the filet thickly.

GORGONZOLA SAUCE

MAKES 3 CUPS

It seems unlikely that you can boil cream and not have it curdle. I was rushing to a party we were catering and the chef had forgotten to make a sauce for the filet. She handed me a quart of heavy cream and told me to boil it for an hour, then add the flavorings. I thought she was crazy, but it turned out to be the easiest sauce I'd ever made. This sauce is flavored with Gorgonzola, but you can use mustard and horseradish instead.

4 cups	heavy cream
3 to 4 ounces	crumbly Gorgonzola (not creamy or "dolce")
3 tablespoons	freshly grated Parmesan cheese
¾ teaspoon	kosher salt
¾ teaspoon	freshly ground black pepper
3 tablespoons	minced fresh parsley

You can use any kind of flavorful, crumbly blue cheese instead of Gorgonzola, such as Maytag blue or Roquefort.

Bring the heavy cream to a full boil in a medium saucepan over medium-high heat, then continue to boil rapidly for 45 to 50 minutes, until it's thickened, like a white sauce, stirring occasionally.

Remove the pan from the heat and add the Gorgonzola, Parmesan, salt, pepper, and parsley. Whisk rapidly until the cheeses melt, and then serve. If you must reheat, warm the sauce over low heat until melted, then whisk vigorously until the sauce comes together.

ROASTED CHERRY TOMATOES

SERVES 8

At Barefoot Contessa we roast lots of vegetables at high temperature. It seems to bring out the sweetness and caramelize the outside a bit. Cherry tomatoes are easy because they don't even need to be peeled.

4 pints	cherry tomatoes
	Good olive oil
	Kosher salt
	Freshly ground black pepper
20	fresh basil leaves, cut into chiffonade
	Sea salt or fleur de sel

Preheat the oven to 400 degrees.

Toss the tomatoes lightly with olive oil on a baking sheet. Spread them out into one layer and sprinkle generously with kosher salt and pepper. Roast for 15 to 20 minutes, until the tomatoes are soft.

Transfer the tomatoes to a serving platter and sprinkle with basil leaves and sea salt. Serve hot or at room temperature.

It's fun to mix red, yellow, and orange cherry tomatoes as well as pear-shaped tomatoes for this dish.

GARLIC ROASTED
POTATOES
SERVES 8

This has to be one of the first vegetables we ever made at Barefoot Contessa, and we haven't stopped since. I can't even begin to calculate how many millions of bags of potatoes we've cooked in the past twenty-three years. But summer or winter, these potatoes always fly out the door. We even make roasted potato soup with the leftovers.

3 pounds	small red- or white-skinned potatoes (or a mixture)
¼ cup	good olive oil
1½ teaspoons	kosher salt
1 teaspoon	freshly ground black pepper
2 tablespoons	minced garlic (6 cloves)
2 tablespoons	minced fresh parsley

At Barefoot Contessa we don't even bother with a bowl. We toss all the ingredients directly on a baking sheet.

You can cut the potatoes the day before and store them covered with water in the refrigerator.

Preheat the oven to 400 degrees.

Cut the potatoes in half or quarters and place in a bowl with the olive oil, salt, pepper, and garlic; toss until the potatoes are well coated. Dump the potatoes on a baking sheet and spread out into one layer; roast in the oven for at least 1 hour, or until browned and crisp. Flip twice with a spatula during cooking to ensure even browning.

Remove the potatoes from the oven, toss with the minced parsley, season to taste, and serve.

CHOCOLATE GANACHE CAKE

MAKES ONE 8-INCH CAKE

This foolproof recipe comes from Devon Fredericks and Susan Costner, who wrote the first Loaves and Fishes Cookbook *in 1978. You can make this fabulous cake up to a week in advance. Wrap it tightly with plastic and refrigerate. Glaze it the day you serve it. We've made this cake into everything from bite-sized cupcakes to wedding cakes for 600 people.*

¼ pound	unsalted butter at room temperature
1 cup	sugar
4	extra-large eggs at room temperature
1	16-ounce can Hershey's chocolate syrup
1 tablespoon	pure vanilla extract
1 cup	all-purpose flour

FOR THE GANACHE

½ cup	heavy cream
8 ounces	good semisweet chocolate chips
1 teaspoon	instant coffee granules
	Candied violets or edible gold leaf, for decoration (optional)

Preheat the oven to 325 degrees. Butter and flour a 8-inch round cake pan, then line the bottom with parchment paper.

Cream the butter and sugar in the bowl of an electric mixer fitted with the paddle attachment until light and fluffy. Add the eggs, one at a time. Mix in the chocolate syrup and vanilla. Add the flour and mix until *just* combined. Don't overbeat, or the cake will be tough.

Pour the batter into the pan and bake for 40 to 45 minutes, or until just set in the middle. Don't overbake! Let cool thoroughly in the pan.

For the ganache, cook the heavy cream, chocolate chips, and instant coffee in the top of a double boiler over simmering water until smooth and warm, stirring occasionally.

Place the cake upside down on a wire rack and pour the glaze evenly over the top, making sure to cover the entire cake and sides. You can tilt the rack to smooth the glaze. Decorate with candied violets, if desired, or gently crumble the gold leaf and place it on the center of the cake. Do not refrigerate.

SUMMER PARTIES

A Party for Twelve

Shrimp Salad

Chinese Chicken Salad

CANOE TRIP

Pasta, Pesto, and Peas

Panzanella

Lemon Cake

ORGANIZE LIKE A CATERER

One of the first things I learned in catering is that good organization is invaluable. I knew that I could make spectacular food, but if the rental company forgot to send forks, the whole evening was a disaster. It was my responsibility to be sure that every detail was perfect and that the flow of the party was seamless. Inevitably, there is always something to deal with—the electricity goes out in the house, the band gets stuck in traffic—but if you're organized you'll be able to deal with it and the guests will *never* know there was a crisis.

When I have parties at home, I literally take a page from my catering experience to organize everything. As a caterer, I had a notebook of blank forms where I would write all the information I needed for each party on one page. At home, I have a similar form with the date of the party, the hours, the guest list, the menu, the liquor and mixers, the service (if any), the table settings, plus any rentals I'll need.

A week before the party, I try out the table settings to be sure I have enough plates for everyone and the silver is polished, the napkins are pressed, and the glasses are sparkling clean. I'm more creative when I'm relaxed, so that's when I decide what flowers or fruit I want to order to make the table look gorgeous. Then I plan what platters I need for each dish on the menu, and I stick a Post-it note on each one. When dinner is hot and friends are coming to the table is *not* the time to come up one platter short.

My ultimate goal in planning is to be a guest at my own party. Even if the party is a summer picnic in canoes around the pond and it looks very informal, having a good plan can make the difference between total fun and total chaos. In the end, I keep these notebook pages as a record of parties I've given, not just for future reference but as a memory book of great times I've had with my friends.

SHRIMP SALAD
SERVES 12

The key to good shrimp salad is to undercook the shrimp. I know it sounds amazing, but they really do cook in 3 minutes. This salad makes a delicious lunch on its own, a first course for dinner, or a great sandwich filling. The old wives' tale about mayonnaise spoiling on a picnic is false; it's the shrimp that spoils, so be sure all your ingredients are cold before you mix them.

3 tablespoons	kosher salt plus 1 teaspoon
1	lemon, cut into quarters
4 pounds	large shrimp in the shell (16 to 20 shrimp per pound)
2 cups	good mayonnaise
1 teaspoon	Dijon mustard
2 tablespoons	good white wine or white wine vinegar
1 teaspoon	freshly ground black pepper
6 tablespoons	minced fresh dill
1 cup	minced red onion (1 onion)
3 cups	minced celery (6 stalks)

Chinese take-out containers are a great way to pack a picnic.

Bring 5 quarts of water, 3 tablespoons salt, and the lemon to a boil in a large saucepan. Add half the shrimp and reduce the heat to medium. Cook, uncovered, for only 3 minutes, or until the shrimp are barely cooked through. Remove with a slotted spoon to a bowl of cool water. Bring the water back to a boil and repeat with the remaining shrimp. Let cool, then peel and devein the shrimp.

In a separate bowl, whisk together the mayonnaise, mustard, wine, 1 teaspoon salt, the pepper, and dill. Combine with the peeled shrimp. Add the red onion and celery and check the seasonings. Serve, or cover and refrigerate for a few hours.

CHINESE CHICKEN SALAD
SERVES 12

I've tested every conceivable way to cook chicken for chicken salad, and this method wins hands-down. I oven-roast bone-in chicken breasts for 35 to 40 minutes, then shred the meat to make the salad. It's moist and flavorful and really absorbs the sauce. This Chinese chicken salad has peanut butter in the dressing to give the flavor depth.

8	split chicken breasts (bone in, skin on)
	Good olive oil
	Kosher salt
	Freshly ground black pepper
1 pound	asparagus, ends removed, cut into thirds diagonally
2	red bell peppers, cored and seeded
4	scallions (white and green parts), sliced diagonally
2 tablespoons	white sesame seeds, toasted

FOR THE DRESSING

1 cup	vegetable oil
¼ cup	good apple cider vinegar
⅓ cup	soy sauce
3 tablespoons	dark sesame oil
1 tablespoon	honey
2	garlic cloves, minced
1 teaspoon	peeled, grated fresh ginger
1 tablespoon	white sesame seeds, toasted
½ cup	smooth peanut butter
4 teaspoons	kosher salt
1 teaspoon	freshly ground black pepper

To toast sesame seeds, place them in a dry sauté pan and cook over medium heat for about 5 minutes, or until browned.

Preheat the oven to 350 degrees.

Place the chicken breasts on a sheet pan and rub the skin with olive oil. Sprinkle liberally with salt and pepper. Roast for 35 to

40 minutes, until the chicken is just cooked. Set aside until cool enough to handle.

Remove the meat from the bones, discard the skin, and shred the chicken in large, bite-sized pieces.

Blanch the asparagus in a pot of boiling salted water for 3 to 5 minutes, until crisp-tender. Plunge into ice water to stop the cooking. Drain. Cut the peppers into strips about the size of the asparagus pieces. Combine the shredded chicken, asparagus, and peppers in a large bowl.

Whisk together all of the ingredients for the dressing and pour over the chicken and vegetables. Add the scallions and sesame seeds and season to taste. Serve cold or at room temperature.

PASTA, PESTO, AND PEAS
SERVES 12

This famous Barefoot Contessa recipe originally came from my wonderful friend Brent Newsom. In order to keep the pesto from turning brown, he adds spinach and lemon juice. To make a delicious and easy one-dish summer lunch, use your imagination and add grilled chicken or fresh salmon.

¾ pound	fusilli pasta
¾ pound	bow-tie pasta
¼ cup	good olive oil
1½ cups	homemade pesto (page 142)
1	10-ounce package frozen chopped spinach, defrosted and squeezed dry
3 tablespoons	freshly squeezed lemon juice
1¼ cups	good mayonnaise
½ cup	grated Parmesan cheese
1½ cups	frozen peas, defrosted
⅓ cup	pignolis, toasted (optional)
¾ teaspoon	kosher salt
¾ teaspoon	freshly ground black pepper

Cook the fusilli and bow ties separately in a large pot of boiling salted water for 10 to 12 minutes, until each pasta is al dente. Drain and toss into a bowl with the olive oil. Cool to room temperature.

In the bowl of a food processor fitted with a steel blade, purée the pesto, spinach, and lemon juice. Add the mayonnaise and continue to purée.

Add the pesto mixture to the cooled pasta, then add the Parmesan cheese, peas, pignolis, salt, and pepper. Mix well, season to taste, and serve at room temperature.

To toast pignolis, place them in a dry sauté pan and cook over medium heat for about 4 minutes, until evenly browned, tossing frequently.

PANZANELLA

This salad was invented by Italians to use up leftover bread, but I make it because I love the warm croutons soaking up the vinaigrette.

3 tablespoons	good olive oil
1	small French bread or boule, cut into 1-inch cubes (6 cups)
1 teaspoon	kosher salt
2	large, ripe tomatoes, cut into 1-inch cubes
1	hothouse cucumber, unpeeled, seeded, and sliced ½ inch thick
1	red bell pepper, seeded and cut into 1-inch cubes
1	yellow bell pepper, seeded and cut into 1-inch cubes
½	red onion, cut in half and thinly sliced
20	large basil leaves, coarsely chopped
3 tablespoons	capers, drained

FOR THE VINAIGRETTE

1 teaspoon	finely minced garlic
½ teaspoon	Dijon mustard
3 tablespoons	champagne vinegar
½ cup	good olive oil
½ teaspoon	kosher salt
¼ teaspoon	freshly ground black pepper

Heat the oil in a large sauté pan. Add the bread and salt; cook over low to medium heat, tossing frequently, for 10 minutes, or until nicely browned. Add more oil as needed.

For the vinaigrette, whisk together the ingredients.

In a large bowl, mix the tomatoes, cucumber, red pepper, yellow pepper, red onion, basil, and capers. Add the bread cubes and toss with the vinaigrette. Season liberally with salt and pepper. Serve, or allow the salad to sit for about half an hour for the flavors to blend.

LEMON CAKE

MAKES TWO 8-INCH LOAVES

A photograph of this lemon cake in The Barefoot Contessa Cookbook *prompted dozens of people to request the recipe. Here it is! This is such a versatile cake. I like to serve it with Lemon Curd (page 203) and fresh raspberries or with Oven-Roasted Fruit (page 117). But a slice with a cup of tea in the afternoon is also just fine with me.*

½ pound	unsalted butter at room temperature
2½ cups	granulated sugar
4	extra-large eggs at room temperature
⅓ cup	grated lemon zest (6 to 8 large lemons)
3 cups	all-purpose flour
½ teaspoon	baking powder
½ teaspoon	baking soda
1 teaspoon	kosher salt
¾ cup	freshly squeezed lemon juice
¾ cup	buttermilk at room temperature
1 teaspoon	pure vanilla extract

FOR THE GLAZE

2 cups	confectioners' sugar, sifted
3½ tablespoons	freshly squeezed lemon juice

Preheat the oven to 350 degrees. Grease, flour, and line the bottom of two 8½ × 4¼ × 2½-inch loaf pans with parchment paper.

Cream the butter and 2 cups granulated sugar in the bowl of an electric mixer fitted with the paddle attachment, for about 5 minutes, or until light and fluffy. With the mixer on medium speed, add the eggs, one at a time, and the lemon zest.

Sift together the flour, baking powder, baking soda, and salt in a bowl. In another bowl, combine ¼ cup lemon juice, the buttermilk, and vanilla. Add the flour and buttermilk mixtures alternately to the batter, beginning and ending with the flour. Divide the batter evenly between the pans, smooth the tops, and bake for 45 minutes to 1 hour, until a cake tester comes out clean.

Combine ½ cup granulated sugar with ½ cup lemon juice in a small saucepan and cook over low heat until the sugar dissolves.

When the cakes are done, let them cool for 10 minutes, then invert them onto a rack set over a tray, and spoon the lemon syrup over the cakes. Allow the cakes to cool completely.

For the glaze, combine the confectioners' sugar and lemon juice in a bowl, mixing with a wire whisk until smooth. Pour over the top of the cakes and allow the glaze to drizzle down the sides.

A Party for Eight

Grilled Leg of Lamb

Hummus*

Tabbouleh

Tzatziki

Tomatoes

LUNCH IN THE
GARDEN

Feta

Sliced Cucumbers

Greek Olives

Green Salad

Pita Breads

Oven-Roasted Fruit

* *The Barefoot Contessa Cookbook*, page 46

ASSEMBLING SANDWICHES

When I think of summer parties, I think of the time long ago when my husband and I were on a camping trip in Provence. We watched a French family eating lunch on a terrace overlooking the Mediterranean. My memory is that everyone was seated at a long table; they were all dressed in white, and big white market umbrellas shaded them from the afternoon sun. Everyone was talking at once, and they were clearly having lots of fun. All Mediterranean cultures —French, Italian, Greek—love to eat al fresco, or outdoors, and the summer weather makes me want to re-create that lunch. I put everything out on a big table and let my friends just help themselves: baskets of fresh breads; plates of prosciutto di Parma; platters of sliced tomatoes, mozzarella, and basil; marinated olives; big wedges of Brie; plus a platter of fresh melons and figs for dessert. There's absolutely nothing to cook! But how good it is.

This party is designed like a Greek lunch al fresco. I drag the dining room table out to the garden, where we can catch the summer breezes. Earlier in the day, I'll grill an herb-marinated butterflied leg of lamb to be put out, sliced, with baskets of pita bread and salads such as tzatziki (a cucumber yogurt salad) and tabbouleh (a spicy wheat salad). All I need to add are bowls of gorgeous sliced cucumbers, tomato wedges, shards of good feta cheese, and maybe a green salad. We all take pita bread and fill it with our favorite ingredients.

The best parties at my house happen when everyone is involved in the meal. Platters are being passed, someone is serving wine, and lunch goes on for hours. This menu is one of my favorites, but be creative and add any Mediterranean ingredients you like.

GRILLED LEG OF LAMB

SERVES 8 TO 12

This is a classic summer dish that was developed by Rori Spinelli. Be sure the lamb is the highest quality, and make your life easy; ask the butcher to butterfly it for you. The grilled lamb should be crusty on the outside and tender and juicy on the inside.

2 pounds	plain yogurt (regular or low-fat)
½ cup	good olive oil, plus more for brushing grill
	Zest of 1 lemon
½ cup	freshly squeezed lemon juice (3 lemons)
¾ cup	fresh whole rosemary leaves (2 large bunches)
2 teaspoons	kosher salt
1 teaspoon	freshly ground black pepper
1	5-pound butterflied leg of lamb (9 pounds bone-in)

Combine the yogurt, olive oil, lemon zest and juice, rosemary, salt, and pepper in a large, nonreactive bowl. Add the lamb, making sure it is covered with the marinade. Marinate in the refrigerator overnight or up to 3 days.

My ideal sandwich: lamb, tomato, cucumber, and tzatziki in pita bread.

Bring the lamb to room temperature. Prepare a charcoal grill with hot coals. Scrape the marinade off the lamb, wipe the meat with paper towels, and season it generously with salt and pepper. Brush the grill with oil to keep the lamb from sticking, and grill on both sides until the internal temperature is 120 to 125 degrees for rare. This will take 40 minutes to an hour, depending on how hot the grill is.

Remove the lamb to a cutting board, cover with aluminum foil, and allow to rest for 20 minutes. Then slice and serve.

TABBOULEH
SERVES 8

This is my idea of not *cooking! You pour boiling water over the bulgur, then add the rest of the ingredients. There's no wondering, Is it done? Is it not done? You can serve this tabbouleh as part of a buffet, but it's also delicious as a summer salad with grilled fish or chicken. It serves eight in pita sandwiches or six to eight as a side dish with dinner.*

1 cup	bulgur wheat
1½ cups	boiling water
¼ cup	freshly squeezed lemon juice (2 lemons)
¼ cup	good olive oil
3½ teaspoons	kosher salt
1 cup	minced scallions, white and green parts (1 bunch)
1 cup	chopped fresh mint leaves (1 bunch)
1 cup	chopped flat-leaf parsley (1 bunch)
1	hothouse cucumber, unpeeled, seeded, and medium-diced
2 cups	cherry tomatoes, cut in half
1 teaspoon	freshly ground black pepper

Place the bulgur in a large bowl, pour in the boiling water, and add the lemon juice, olive oil, and 1½ teaspoons salt. Stir, then allow to stand at room temperature for about an hour.

Add the scallions, mint, parsley, cucumber, tomatoes, 2 teaspoons salt, and the pepper; mix well. Season to taste and serve, or cover and refrigerate. The flavor will improve if the tabbouleh sits for a few hours.

Bulgur is an exceptionally nutritious wheat grain that is popular in the Middle East.

TZATZIKI

MAKES 5 CUPS

This appetizer is easy to assemble, although it takes a bit of planning. But oh! is it worth the wait. As part of a light summer meal it is a cool and satisfying salad; it's also terrific with pita as a dip. It can be prepared days ahead of time.

4 cups	plain yogurt, whole milk or low-fat
2	hothouse cucumbers, unpeeled and seeded
2 tablespoons	plus 1 teaspoon kosher salt
1 cup	sour cream
2 tablespoons	champagne vinegar or white wine vinegar
¼ cup	freshly squeezed lemon juice (2 lemons)
2 tablespoons	good olive oil
1 tablespoon	minced garlic (2 cloves)
1 tablespoon	minced fresh dill
¼ teaspoon	freshly ground black pepper

Good-quality, plain white paper towels can be used instead of cheesecloth.

Place the yogurt in a cheesecloth-lined sieve and set it over a bowl. Grate the cucumber and toss it with 2 tablespoons salt; place it in another sieve and set it over another bowl. Place both bowls in the refrigerator for 3 to 4 hours so the yogurt and cucumber can drain.

Transfer the thickened yogurt to a large bowl. Squeeze as much liquid from the cucumbers as you can and add the cucumbers to the yogurt. Mix in the sour cream, vinegar, lemon juice, olive oil, garlic, dill, 1 teaspoon salt, and pepper. You can serve it immediately, but I prefer to allow the tzatziki to sit in the refrigerator for a few hours for the flavors to blend.

OVEN-ROASTED
FRUIT
SERVES 8

This is a wonderful and versatile dessert. I love to serve it warm with a dollop of crème fraîche, but it is also delicious at room temperature over vanilla ice cream or on a slice of Lemon Cake (page 104). My friend Johanne Killeen made a dessert like this at her romantic house in Provence, and I couldn't wait to get home to make it, too.

6	peaches, pitted and cut into eighths
6	plums or Italian prune plums, pitted and halved or quartered
½ cup	sugar
2 cups	fresh raspberries
2 tablespoons	orange juice

Preheat the oven to 450 degrees.

Place the peaches and plums snugly in a single layer, cut-side up, in two glass or porcelain ovenproof baking dishes. Sprinkle with the sugar, and then add the raspberries. Bake for 20 to 25 minutes, until tender.

Heat the broiler and place the fruit about 5 inches below the heat and broil for 5 to 8 minutes until the berries release some of their juices.

Remove from the broiler and sprinkle with the orange juice. Serve warm, at room temperature, or chilled.

You can use all kinds of soft fruit: figs, nectarines, papaya, mango, blueberries, or blackberries.

A Party for Six

Balsamic Onions and Blue Cheese

Asian Grilled Salmon

HAPPY BIRTHDAY!

Sautéed Fresh Corn

Sautéed Asparagus and Snap Peas

Strawberry Country Cake

INSPIRATION FROM THE SEASON

Everyone knows that chefs go to the market and see what's fresh before deciding what to cook. Their menus change daily and are based on whatever is in season. I call this "cooking from ingredients." On the other hand, most of us decide what we want to eat, find a recipe that pleases us, then go to the market to find the ingredients for that recipe. We might make fresh corn salad in summer or onion soup in winter, but a special ingredient isn't the compelling reason to choose a particular dish. You can change that.

At Barefoot Contessa we make lots of dishes year-round because customers love them, but I am often inspired to make something because a special ingredient has just become available in the market: sugar snap peas and asparagus in summer, for example, or fingerling potatoes and sweet onions in fall. In June, the strawberries are plentiful and fragrant at the farm stands, and I'm dying to make strawberry country cakes and fresh strawberry jam. In autumn, the apples and pears are ripe and I can't wait to make old-fashioned crisps.

The key to cooking from ingredients is using a few basic recipes and techniques. One such technique is oven roasting at high temperature. I use the same technique for all kinds of firm vegetables: carrots, fennel, potatoes, peppers, Brussels sprouts—whatever looks the best. When more tender vegetables—corn, sugar snap peas, asparagus, or cabbage—are available, I turn to sautéing in a bit of butter and oil. And a basic pound cake is a perfect vehicle for lots of the fruits and berries of summer. With versatile recipes, I can go to the market and see what looks good, and my friends will have delicious meals made from the best the season has to offer.

BALSAMIC ONIONS
AND BLUE CHEESE

Nick & Toni's has been my favorite restaurant in East Hampton ever since Jeff Salaway and Toni Ross opened it in 1988. This is a salad they make from time to time, and I love the sweet onions with the sharp blue cheese.

3	small red onions
¼ cup	plus 2 tablespoons good balsamic vinegar
1 cup	good olive oil
1½ teaspoons	kosher salt
1 teaspoon	freshly ground black pepper
6 tablespoons	minced shallots (2 large)
2 teaspoons	Dijon mustard
¼ cup	good red wine vinegar
¾ to 1 pound	Maytag blue cheese, or other crumbly blue
2 heads	red-leaf lettuce, washed, spun dry, and torn

Preheat the oven to 375 degrees.

Cut the onions in half and slice ¼ inch thick. Place on a baking sheet and toss with ¼ cup balsamic vinegar, ¼ cup olive oil, 1 teaspoon salt, and ½ teaspoon pepper. Bake for 12 to 15 minutes, until the onions are tender. Remove from the oven, toss with 2 more tablespoons balsamic vinegar, and let cool to room temperature.

To make the dressing, whisk the shallots, mustard, red wine vinegar, ½ teaspoon salt, and ½ teaspoon pepper in a small bowl. While whisking, add ¾ cup olive oil until the dressing is emulsified. Mash ¼ pound blue cheese with a fork and add it to the dressing.

To assemble, toss enough lettuce for 6 people with dressing to taste. Place the lettuce on 6 plates and arrange the onions on top. Coarsely crumble the rest of the blue cheese on top. Sprinkle with salt and pepper and serve.

ASIAN GRILLED
SALMON

I actually spent a whole summer grilling salmon in all sorts of ways in order to master the technique. Two things made a big difference in the flavor: first, a simple marinade that I spooned on the salmon before grilling and after it was done, and second, taking the salmon off the grill before it was finished cooking. I grill extra salmon so I can serve it for dinner one night and in a salad or in sandwiches the next day.

1 side	fresh salmon, boned but skin on (about 3 pounds)

FOR THE MARINADE

2 tablespoons	Dijon mustard
3 tablespoons	good soy sauce
6 tablespoons	good olive oil
½ teaspoon	minced garlic

Light charcoal briquettes in a grill and brush the grilling rack with oil to keep the salmon from sticking.

While the grill is heating, lay the salmon skin-side down on a cutting board and cut it crosswise into 6 equal pieces. Whisk together the mustard, soy sauce, olive oil, and garlic in a small bowl. Drizzle half of the marinade onto the salmon and allow it to sit for 10 minutes.

Place the salmon skin-side down on the hot grill; discard the marinade the fish was sitting in. Grill for 4 to 5 minutes, depending on the thickness of the fish. Turn carefully with a wide spatula and grill for another 4 to 5 minutes. The salmon will be slightly raw in the center, but don't worry; it will keep cooking as it sits.

Transfer the fish to a flat plate, skin-side down, and spoon the reserved marinade on top. Allow the fish to rest for 10 minutes. Remove the skin and serve warm, at room temperature, or chilled.

SAUTÉED FRESH CORN

SERVES 6 TO 8

When my wonderful friend cookbook writer and teacher Patricia Wells came to visit me in East Hampton from her home in Paris, the first thing she wanted to do was hit the farm stands. It was August and the corn was tender and sweet. We cut the corn off the cob and ate sautéed corn every day.

8 ears	corn on the cob
3 tablespoons	unsalted butter
1 teaspoon	kosher salt
¼ teaspoon	freshly ground black pepper

Remove the husks and silk from the corn and cut off the kernels as close to the cob as possible. You should have about 7 cups of kernels.

Melt the butter in a large, heavy sauté pan over medium-low heat. Add the corn, salt, and pepper and sauté, uncovered, for 8 to 10 minutes, stirring occasionally, until all the starchiness in the corn is gone. Taste for salt and pepper and serve.

You can mix 1½ tablespoons butter with 1½ tablespoons olive oil to get the flavor of butter and the high burning point of olive oil.

SAUTÉED ASPARAGUS AND SNAP PEAS

SERVES 6 TO 8

Asparagus can be handled like cut flowers; to store them in the refrigerator, cut off the tough ends and stand them upright in a glass of water. Asparagus is in season in early summer with sugar snap peas, so I often sauté them together. Sprinkle them with a little sea salt just before serving.

2 pounds	asparagus
1½ pounds	sugar snap peas
2 tablespoons	good olive oil
	Kosher salt
	Freshly ground black pepper
	Red pepper flakes (optional)
	Sea salt for serving (optional)

Cut off the tough ends of the asparagus and slice the stalks diagonally into 2-inch pieces. Snap off the stem ends of the snap peas and pull the string down the length of the vegetable.

If the asparagus stalks are thick, I peel them.

Warm the olive oil in a large sauté pan over medium-high heat and add the asparagus and snap peas. Add kosher salt, pepper, and red pepper flakes, if desired, to taste. Cook for approximately 10 minutes, or until crisp-tender, tossing occasionally. Sprinkle with sea salt, if desired, and serve hot.

STRAWBERRY COUNTRY CAKE

MAKES TWO 8-INCH CAKES
EACH CAKE SERVES 6 TO 8

This is the most delicious cake to make when strawberries are in season. The recipe makes two 8-inch cakes. If you are not using the second cake, let it cool completely, wrap in plastic, and freeze for up to 6 months.

¾ cup	unsalted butter (1½ sticks) at room temperature
2 cups	sugar
4	extra-large eggs at room temperature
¾ cup	sour cream at room temperature
½ teaspoon	grated lemon zest
½ teaspoon	grated orange zest
½ teaspoon	pure vanilla extract
2 cups	all-purpose flour
¼ cup	cornstarch
½ teaspoon	kosher salt
1 teaspoon	baking soda

FOR THE FILLING FOR *EACH* CAKE

1 cup	heavy whipping cream (½ pint), chilled
3 tablespoons	sugar
½ teaspoon	pure vanilla extract
1 pint	fresh strawberries, hulled and sliced

Preheat the oven to 350 degrees. Butter and flour two 8-inch cake pans.

Cream the butter and sugar on high speed until light and fluffy in the bowl of an electric mixer fitted with a paddle attachment. On medium speed, add the eggs, one at a time, then the sour cream, zests, and vanilla, scraping down the bowl as needed. Mix well. Sift together the flour, cornstarch, salt, and baking soda. On low speed, slowly add the flour mixture to the butter mixture and combine just until smooth.

Pour the batter evenly into the pans, smooth the tops with a spatula, and bake in the center of the oven for 40 to 45 minutes, until a toothpick comes out clean. Let cool in the pans for 30 minutes, then remove to wire racks and let cool to room temperature.

To make the filling for *one* cake, whip the cream by hand or in a mixer until firm; add the sugar and vanilla. Slice one of the cakes in half with a long, sharp knife. Place the bottom slice of the cake on a serving platter, spread with half of the whipped cream, and scatter with sliced strawberries. Cover with the top slice of the cake and spread with the remaining cream. Decorate with strawberries.

A Party for Six

Real Margaritas

Endive and Avocado Salad

OUTDOOR GRILL

Grilled Herb Shrimp with Mango Salsa

Spaghettoni al Pesto

Tomato Fennel Salad

Peach Raspberry Shortcakes

THE BOSS COMES TO DINNER

When my husband was an investment banker, we often entertained —his boss, clients, other bankers, and some old friends from his previous job at the State Department. The group tended to be fairly stuffy, so I would plan relaxed menus to loosen everyone up. Whenever our guests tend to be formal, I love to serve casual food, particularly things that need to be eaten with your hands. In my first book, I wrote about serving a huge kitchen clambake. But I also make fried chicken, ribs, and big chunks of corn bread that we eat with our fingers. Guests always go home saying, "Wasn't that fun!"

Disaster struck fifteen minutes before one memorable party in our New York City loft. Both elevators broke down, and I realized that the guests, including Jeffrey's former boss, Secretary of State Cyrus Vance, would have to walk up eleven flights of stairs. I knew that the only thing worse for the guests than walking up all those stairs was for me to be upset when they arrived, so I greeted everybody with big iced margaritas and made them feel as welcome as possible.

I was glad that I had planned earthy food for this party. The menu of grilled shrimp and pasta pesto was relaxed enough to make sure that the men would take off their business jackets, roll up their sleeves, and dig in. It turned out to be one of the liveliest parties I've ever had. People had actually bonded on the trek upstairs!

Of course, you don't have to serve this menu only in formal situations, but I like it when friends don't know what to expect when they come to my house. Because most of these dishes can be prepared in advance, you, too, can have fun at your party.

REAL MARGARITAS

SERVES 6

My assistant Barbara Libath and I were on our twelfth version of margaritas (not a terrible job) when my friends Gilberto Carranzo and Alejandro Silva came by. They're from Mexico, they're terrific cooks, and they showed us how to make real *margaritas. None of us got too much more work done that day. The keys to this recipe are to use fresh lime juice and* inexpensive *tequila.*

1	lime, halved
	Kosher salt
½ cup	freshly squeezed lime juice (5 limes)
2 tablespoons	freshly squeezed lemon juice (1 lemon)
1 cup	Triple Sec
3 cups	ice
1 cup	white tequila

I use lots of different salts. Clockwise from top left: kosher salt, fleur de sel, flaked sea salt, and fine sea salt. Use kosher salt for margaritas.

If you like margaritas served in a glass with salt, rub the outside rims of six glasses with a cut lime and dip each glass lightly into a plate of kosher salt.

Combine the lime juice, lemon juice, Triple Sec, and ice in a blender and purée until completely blended. Add the tequila and puree for 2 seconds more. Serve over ice.

If you prefer frozen margaritas (photograph on page 11), halve each of the ingredients, double the ice, and blend in two batches. Serve with a cut lime.

ENDIVE AND
AVOCADO SALAD
SERVES 6

This recipe is inspired by a salad I love at E.A.T. in New York City. Because endive and avocados are delicious year-round, you can make this as a first course anytime. It's also a great salad for a crowd, because no cooking is needed, and the lemon juice keeps the avocados green.

1½ tablespoons	Dijon mustard
¼ cup	freshly squeezed lemon juice (2 lemons)
4 to 5 tablespoons	good olive oil
¾ teaspoon	kosher salt
½ teaspoon	freshly ground black pepper
4	heads of endive
4	ripe Hass avocados, peeled and seeded

Whisk together the mustard, lemon juice, olive oil, salt, and pepper to make a vinaigrette.

Remove a half inch from the stem end of each endive, discard the core, and cut the rest across into 1-inch chunks. Cut the avocados into large dice or wedges. Toss the avocados and endive with the vinaigrette. Season to taste and serve at room temperature.

Hass avocados are the brown ones from California. The green ones don't have nearly as much flavor.

GRILLED HERB SHRIMP
SERVES 6

I'm a charter member of the Craig Claiborne fan club. He taught us all how to make wonderful meals with common ingredients. This is a slight variation of a recipe from his original New York Times Cookbook, and I've been making it for years. It's great for dinner, but I also make it for an appetizer at cocktail parties.

3	garlic cloves, minced
1	medium yellow onion, small-diced
¼ cup	minced fresh parsley
¼ cup	minced fresh basil
1 teaspoon	dry mustard
2 teaspoons	Dijon mustard
2 teaspoons	kosher salt
¼ teaspoon	freshly ground black pepper
¼ cup	good olive oil
	Juice of 1 lemon
2 pounds	jumbo shrimp (16 to 20 per pound), peeled (tails left on) and deveined
	Mango Salsa (recipe follows)

For cocktails, place each shrimp on its own 6-inch skewer and cook the same way. This recipe makes enough for 8 to 10 people for cocktails.

You can also broil the shrimp: 3 inches from the flame and 2 minutes per side.

Combine the garlic, onion, parsley, basil, mustards, salt, pepper, olive oil, and lemon juice. Add the shrimp and allow them to marinate for 1 hour at room temperature or cover and refrigerate for up to 2 days.

Prepare a charcoal grill with hot coals, and brush the grilling rack with oil to prevent the shrimp from sticking. Skewer the shrimp. I use 5 or 6 shrimp on a 12-inch skewer for a dinner serving. Grill the shrimp for 1½ minutes on each side. Serve with the Mango Salsa.

MANGO SALSA

MAKES 2 CUPS

Parker Hodges is my partner and the chef at Barefoot Contessa. He grew up in Nicaragua, and he makes this scrumptious fresh salsa. It's sweet, spicy, and chunky and it's wonderful for dinner with Grilled Herb Shrimp (page 138).

2 tablespoons	good olive oil
1½ cups	diced yellow onion (2 onions)
2 teaspoons	peeled, minced fresh ginger
1½ teaspoons	minced garlic
2	ripe mangos, peeled, seeded, and small-diced
⅓ cup	freshly squeezed orange juice
2 teaspoons	light brown sugar
1 teaspoon	kosher salt
½ teaspoon	freshly ground black pepper
1 to 2 teaspoons	minced fresh jalapeño pepper, to taste (1 pepper)
2 teaspoons	minced fresh mint leaves

There's a lot of heat in jalapeño seeds, so be sure you don't get any seeds in the salsa.

Sauté the olive oil, onions, and ginger in a large sauté pan over medium-low heat for 10 minutes, or until the onions are translucent. Add the garlic and cook for 1 more minute. Add the mangos; reduce the heat to low and cook for 10 more minutes. Add the orange juice, brown sugar, salt, black pepper, and jalapeños; cook for 10 more minutes, or until the orange juice is reduced, stirring occasionally.

Remove from the heat and add the mint. Serve warm, at room temperature, or chilled.

SPAGHETTONI AL PESTO

SERVES 6

It seems we all got tired of pesto in the seventies and stopped making it altogether. But in the summer, when the basil is growing wild in my garden and the aroma is so fragrant, I can't resist making lots of this pasta pesto. Spaghettoni is available from specialty markets and Williams-Sonoma, but plain spaghetti is also just fine.

	Good olive oil
	Kosher salt
1 pound	spaghettoni, bucatini, or spaghetti
1 to 1½ cups	pesto (recipe follows)

To clean basil, remove the leaves, swirl them in a bowl of water, and then spin them very dry in a salad spinner. Store them in a closed plastic bag with a slightly damp paper towel. As long as the leaves are dry they will stay green for several days.

Splash some oil in a large pot of salted boiling water and add pasta. Cook the spaghettoni for 10 to 12 minutes, until al dente but cooked through. Drain the pasta in a colander and toss it in a large bowl with enough pesto to coat each strand. Taste for seasoning and serve hot or at room temperature.

PESTO

MAKES 4 CUPS

¼ cup	walnuts
¼ cup	pignolis
3 tablespoons	diced garlic (9 cloves)
5 cups	fresh basil leaves, packed
1 teaspoon	kosher salt
1 teaspoon	freshly ground black pepper
1½ cups	good olive oil
1 cup	freshly grated Parmesan cheese

Place the walnuts, pignolis, and garlic in the bowl of a food processor fitted with a steel blade. Process for 30 seconds. Add the basil leaves, salt, and pepper. With the processor running, slowly pour the

olive oil into the bowl through the feed tube and process until the pesto is finely puréed. Add the Parmesan and purée for a minute. Serve, or store the pesto in the refrigerator or freezer with a thin film of olive oil on top.

TOMATO
FENNEL SALAD
SERVES 6 TO 8

Commercial tomatoes have been hybridized for color and durability, not for flavor. Lots of small growers are finding the old tomato varieties that taste like old-fashioned tomatoes; they're grown from what are called heirloom seeds. If you can't find or grow these tomatoes, use the best you can buy from local farm stands and markets.

1½ pounds	heirloom tomatoes
1	small fennel bulb
2 tablespoons	good olive oil
	Zest of 1 small orange
2 tablespoons	fresh orange juice
1 tablespoon	cider vinegar
1 teaspoon	kosher salt
½ teaspoon	freshly ground black pepper

Core the tomatoes and cut into wedges. Remove the top of the fennel (save some fronds for garnish) and slice the bulb very thinly crosswise with a knife or on a mandoline.

Toss the tomatoes and fennel in a bowl with the olive oil, orange zest, orange juice, vinegar, salt, and pepper. Garnish with 2 tablespoons chopped fennel fronds, season to taste, and serve.

For such a simple recipe, you need the best ingredients. Make this only in summer.

Don't ever refrigerate tomatoes.

PEACH RASPBERRY SHORTCAKES

This recipe says summer every time. Cut out the shortcake dough ahead of time, then egg-wash the rounds and pop them into the oven just before dinner so the house smells wonderful. They're best served just slightly warm, piled high with whipped cream and fruit.

2 cups	all-purpose flour
1 tablespoon	sugar, plus extra for sprinkling
1 tablespoon	baking powder
1 teaspoon	kosher salt
12 tablespoons	cold unsalted butter (1½ sticks), diced
2	extra-large eggs, lightly beaten
½ cup	heavy cream, chilled
1	egg beaten with 2 tablespoons water or milk, for egg wash

TO ASSEMBLE

1 cup	heavy cream, chilled
2 tablespoons	sugar
½ teaspoon	pure vanilla extract
2	ripe peaches, peeled, pitted, and thinly sliced
1 pint	raspberries
	Zest of 1 orange removed in long strips

Preheat the oven to 400 degrees.

Sift the flour, 1 tablespoon sugar, the baking powder, and salt into the bowl of an electric mixer fitted with the paddle attachment. Blend in the butter at the lowest speed and mix until the butter is the size of peas. Combine the eggs and heavy cream and quickly add to the flour and butter mixture. Mix until *just* blended. The dough will be sticky.

(recipe continues on page 148)

Dump the dough out onto a well-floured surface. Flour your hands and pat the dough out ¾ inch thick. You should see lumps of butter in the dough.

Cut 6 or 7 biscuits with a 2¾-inch fluted cutter and place on a baking sheet lined with parchment.

Brush the tops with the egg wash. Sprinkle with sugar and bake for 20 to 25 minutes, until the outsides are crisp and the insides are fully baked. Let cool on a wire rack.

To assemble, whip the cream and sugar in the bowl of an electric mixer fitted with a whisk attachment until soft peaks form. Add the vanilla and continue to beat until the peaks are stiff.

Split each shortcake in half crosswise and place the bottom half on a plate. Spoon whipped cream on top, then place the sliced peaches and raspberries on the whipped cream. Garnish with the orange zest, then place the other half of the shortcake on top and serve.

AUTUMN PARTIES

A Party for Ten

Breadsticks

Popcorn

Salted Cashews

Grilled Salmon Sandwiches

FOOTBALL PARTY

Lobster Rolls

Filet of Beef Sandwiches

Outrageous Brownies★

Caramel Chocolate Nut Ice Cream

Imported Beers

★ *The Barefoot Contessa Cookbook*, page 172

"BEST OF CLASS"

Anyone who knows Martha Stewart, as I have had the good fortune to, knows that she values what I call "best of class." It doesn't matter to her whether we're talking about hot dogs or caviar—she wants to know if something is made with quality. I *love* that notion, and I have always tried to follow it even before I had a name for it. It doesn't matter whether you offer meat loaf or filet of beef at your parties; what matters is that it's the best you can make it and that you serve it with style.

When I have a reason to invite a large group to my house for a party, I try to have some sort of entertainment for them. A lovely dinner with satisfying conversation seems to work best with smaller groups. With a large group, some activity—whether it's a poker game or watching football on television—always seems to get everyone involved. I have a buffet of delicious food so we can all help ourselves and move around. This makes the party more free-wheeling than a traditional sit-down dinner.

But what do you serve during a football game? Sandwiches, of course, but they need to be "best of class." For this party, I made lobster salad on a roll, grilled salmon with herb sauce, and filet of beef with blue cheese. The variety of great sandwiches you can make is limited only by your imagination. From *The Barefoot Contessa Cookbook,* you could make hummus and cucumber on pita, crab cakes on brioche rolls, fresh turkey on raisin nut bread with scallion cream cheese, and smoked salmon sandwiches. From this book, try the roast loin of pork with honey mustard on country bread, and shrimp salad on 7-grain bread. The important thing is to use only the best ingredients—and your best linens. Your friends will *love* eating sandwiches; and you can be a guest at the party, too, since everything's done in advance.

GRILLED SALMON SANDWICHES

SERVES 6

I'm sure this sandwich started life as a way to use leftover salmon, but it's so good, why not make it fresh? The key is to take the salmon off the grill before it's done, as it keeps cooking for a few minutes.

	Good olive oil
2 pounds	fresh salmon fillets, skin-on
	Kosher salt to taste
	Freshly ground black pepper to taste

FOR THE SAUCE

1 cup	good mayonnaise
¼ cup	sour cream
¾ teaspoon	white wine vinegar
12	large fresh basil leaves
¾ cup	chopped fresh dill
1½ tablespoons	chopped scallions, white and green parts
¼ teaspoon	kosher salt
¼ teaspoon	freshly ground black pepper
3 teaspoons	capers, drained

TO ASSEMBLE

6	fresh white or brioche rolls (4-inch rounds)
¼ pound	mesclun mix or fresh basil leaves

For the salmon, prepare a charcoal grill and brush the grilling rack with oil. Rub the outside of the salmon with olive oil, salt, and pepper. Grill the fish for 5 minutes on each side, or until it is *almost* cooked through. Remove to a plate and allow it to rest for 15 minutes. Remove any remaining skin.

For the sauce, place the mayonnaise, sour cream, vinegar, basil, dill, scallions, salt, and pepper in the bowl of a food processor fitted with a steel blade. Process until combined. Add the capers and pulse two or three times.

To assemble the sandwiches, slice the rolls in half crosswise. Spread 1 tablespoon of the sauce on each cut side. Place some mesclun mix or basil on the bottom half, then a piece of salmon. Place the top of the roll on the salmon and serve.

LOBSTER ROLLS

MAKES 7 OR 8 SANDWICHES

A very famous restaurant near East Hampton (I'm sure it has a name, but no one knows it) advertises "lobster roll" for "lunch," so it's alternately called "Lobster Roll" or "Lunch." It's the essence of lunch on the beach even though it's not even on the beach. With this recipe, you can make this treat at home. If lobster is too expensive or unavailable, use lump crabmeat or boiled shrimp instead.

¾ pound	cooked fresh lobster meat, diced
½ cup	good mayonnaise
½ cup	finely diced celery (1½ stalks)
1 tablespoon	capers, drained
1½ tablespoons	finely minced fresh dill
	Pinch of kosher salt
	Pinch of freshly ground black pepper
8	hot dog rolls, grilled or toasted

Combine the lobster, mayonnaise, celery, capers, dill, salt, and pepper. Fill each roll and serve.

I use Pepperidge Farm hot dog rolls, which are split on the top.

FILET OF BEEF
SANDWICHES
MAKES 6 SANDWICHES

At Barefoot Contessa we make lots of wonderful sandwiches every day. Roast beef and blue cheese on health bread is one of my favorites, but I made it more special here with filet of beef. I prefer the small "panini," the kind of sandwich served in Italy, to the big bulky American ones.

FOR THE DRESSING

¼ pound	blue d'Auvergne or other creamy blue cheese
⅔ cup	sour cream
⅓ cup	mayonnaise
1½ teaspoons	Worcestershire sauce
1 teaspoon	kosher salt
1 teaspoon	freshly ground black pepper

TO ASSEMBLE

1 loaf	health or 7-grain bread
1¼ pounds	rare filet of beef (page 82), thinly sliced
1 bunch	arugula
	Kosher salt
	Freshly ground black pepper
2 tablespoons	unsalted butter at room temperature

For the dressing, mash the blue cheese with a fork and blend with the sour cream, mayonnaise, Worcestershire sauce, salt, and pepper.

To make the sandwiches, cut the bread into 12 slices, each slice ¼ inch thick. Spread 6 of the slices thickly with the dressing. Top with slices of beef and arugula and sprinkle with salt and pepper. Spread the rest of the slices of bread very lightly with butter and place, butter-side down, on top of the beef.

CARAMEL CHOCOLATE NUT ICE CREAM
MAKES 2 QUARTS

My friend Barbara Libath's favorite sweets are the caramel, chocolate, and pecan concoctions called "turtles." So we decided to make an ice cream with all those flavors. Boy, was that a mistake. It was so good that we couldn't stop eating it. When I make this for a dinner party, it's always a hit. If you have a one-quart ice cream maker, you will have to freeze the mix in two batches.

2½ cups	sugar
6 cups	heavy cream
2 tablespoons	pure vanilla extract
3 cups	pecan halves (10 ounces)
6 to 7 ounces	best-quality sweet chocolate, diced (see note)

I prefer Lindt Lindor truffles (two 3.5-ounce packages) because they do not freeze hard. Lindt Swiss Milk Chocolate (two 3-ounce packages) or any good milk chocolate is fine, too.

Place ½ cup of water and the sugar in a large, heavy-bottomed saucepan, and cook over low heat, without stirring, until the sugar is dissolved. Increase the heat to high and boil until the sugar turns a warm mahogany or caramel color, 3 to 5 minutes. Do not stir, but swirl the pan occasionally so the caramel cooks evenly.

Remove the caramel from the heat and *carefully* pour in the cream. The caramel is very hot, and the mixture will bubble up violently, then solidify. Don't worry. Return it to low heat and cook, stirring with a wooden spoon, until the caramel dissolves, 5 to 7 minutes. Add the vanilla. Pour into a container and refrigerate until very cold.

Preheat the oven to 350 degrees. Roast the pecans on a baking sheet for 8 to 10 minutes, until crisp. Cool, chop, mix with the diced chocolate, and store in the freezer until ready to use.

Freeze the caramel mixture in an ice cream freezer according to the manufacturer's directions. (It may take several batches.) When it is frozen, add the cold chopped pecans and chocolate and mix in completely. Transfer to quart containers and store in the freezer until ready to serve.

A Party for Six

Potato Pancakes with Caviar

Salad with Warm Goat Cheese

AUTUMN DINNER

Rack of Lamb

Orzo with Roasted Vegetables

Apple Crostata

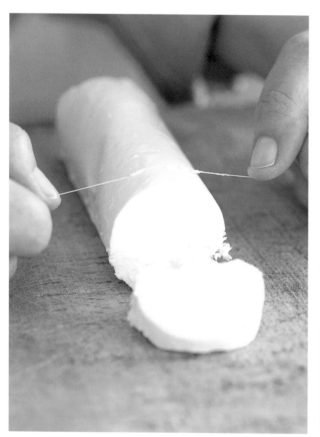 

COOKING TOGETHER

One of my favorite things to do is visit my dear friends Devon Fredericks and Eli Zabar at their house in Provence. We spend the days scouring the nearby food markets for fresh ingredients and the nights cooking in their wood-burning oven. In the late afternoon, we prepare some treat such as the tiny local shellfish called *talines* and eat them with a local white wine while we prepare the rest of the meal together. It's so pleasurable that it makes me weep just to think about it.

When I'm home in East Hampton, I can never really re-create the experience of shopping and cooking in Provence, but I have brought one of Devon and Eli's ideas to my parties: I cook with my guests. Old friends have a wonderful time together, people who don't know one another well connect quickly. Good cooks become the teachers, and people who don't cook are the assistants. Everyone has fun.

Of course, the best news is for the host. Not only does the party start *before* the dinner begins, I don't have to cook all day! All I do in advance is shop for ingredients and set the table. If dinner is for six people and we cook in pairs, a dinner that would take me three hours on my own is done in an hour while we drink wine and snack on potato pancakes and caviar.

This is an easy menu to make with friends. The least experienced cook can make the salad, the most experienced can make the apple crostata (everyone loves to learn how to make flaky pastry), and I'm in charge of the rack of lamb, which takes only about twenty minutes to cook. I hope you'll find that this is such a successful formula for a party that you'll do it again and again.

POTATO PANCAKES
WITH CAVIAR
SERVES 6 TO 8

There's something wonderfully extravagant about putting caviar on an earthy potato pancake. These need to be sautéed the minute before they're eaten, so I make them only when we're all cooking together. Then we have something special to eat while we're getting dinner ready.

4 large	baking potatoes
2	extra-large eggs, whisked
6 tablespoons	all-purpose flour
2½ teaspoons	kosher salt
½ teaspoon	freshly ground black pepper
6 tablespoons	clarified butter (see note)
½ cup	crème fraîche or sour cream
About 3¼ ounces	(100 grams) good caviar or salmon roe

Peel the potatoes and grate them lengthwise. Place them in a colander or kitchen towel and squeeze out as much liquid as possible. Combine the potatoes in a bowl with the eggs, flour, salt, and pepper. Mix well.

Melt 2 tablespoons of the clarified butter in a skillet over medium heat. Drop a tablespoon of the potato mixture into the sizzling butter. Flatten with a spatula and cook for 2 minutes. Turn, flatten again, and cook for another 2 minutes, or until crisp on the outside and golden brown. Serve the pancakes hot from the skillet with a dollop of crème fraîche and a teaspoon of caviar.

To make 6 tablespoons clarified butter, slowly melt 8 tablespoons butter in a small saucepan. Set it aside until the milk solids settle. Spoon off any solids that rise, then carefully pour off the golden liquid, discarding the milky part in the bottom of the pan.

SALAD WITH WARM GOAT CHEESE

SERVES 6

This salad can be an appetizer or a wonderful light lunch on its own. I particularly like the interplay of hot and cold and sweet-tart dressing plus the bite of goat cheese. Serve the salad with crusty bread.

1	11-ounce log of plain or herbed Montrachet
2	extra-large egg whites beaten with
	1 tablespoon water
	Fresh white bread crumbs

FOR THE DRESSING

2 tablespoons	good cider vinegar
2 tablespoons	good champagne vinegar
Pinch	sugar
½ teaspoon	kosher salt, or to taste
¼ teaspoon	freshly ground black pepper
1	extra-large egg yolk (see note)
1 cup	good olive oil

Enough mixed salad greens for 6
Enough olive oil and unsalted butter for frying

For fresh bread crumbs, cut the crusts off white bread, cube it, and pulse in a food processor fitted with a metal blade for 15 seconds, until finely crumbed.

If you are concerned about raw egg yolk, substitute 1 tablespoon of mayonnaise.

Slice the Montrachet into twelve ½-inch-thick slices. (The easiest way to slice goat cheese is to use a length of dental floss.) Dip each slice into the beaten egg whites, then the bread crumbs, being sure the cheese is thoroughly coated. Place the slices on a rack and chill them for at least 15 minutes.

For the dressing, place the vinegars, sugar, salt, pepper, and egg yolk in the bowl of a food processor fitted with a steel blade and blend for 1 minute. With the motor running, slowly pour the olive oil through the feed tube until the vinaigrette is thickened. Season to taste.

Toss the salad greens with enough dressing to moisten, then divide them among 6 plates.

Melt 1 tablespoon oil and 1 tablespoon butter in a sauté pan over medium-high heat until just under smoking. Cook the goat cheese rounds quickly on both sides until browned on the outside but not melted inside. Top each salad with 2 warm rounds and serve.

RACK OF LAMB
SERVES 6

This dish may be expensive, but it's incredibly easy. I made it with friends when we cooked dinner together on the New Year's Eve of the millennium, and I'll always remember it as one of the best meals we'd ever made together. Even the most novice cook will feel like a professional!

1½ tablespoons	kosher salt
2 tablespoons	minced fresh rosemary
3	garlic cloves, minced
½ cup	Dijon mustard
1 tablespoon	balsamic vinegar
2	racks of lamb, "frenched" (see note)

Check the lamb with an instant-read meat thermometer. Rare will be 125 degrees; medium-rare is 130 degrees.

"Frenching" refers to scraping the meat off the tips of the bones. Ask your butcher to leave ⅛ inch of fat on the meat.

In the bowl of a food processor fitted with a steel blade, process the salt, rosemary, and garlic until they're as finely minced as possible. Add the mustard and balsamic vinegar and process for 1 minute.

Place the lamb in a roasting pan with the ribs curving down, and coat the tops with the mustard mixture. Allow to stand for 1 hour at room temperature.

Preheat the oven to 450 degrees.

Roast the lamb for exactly 20 minutes for rare or 25 minutes for medium-rare. Remove from the oven and cover with aluminum foil. Allow to sit for 15 minutes, then cut into individual ribs and serve.

ORZO WITH ROASTED VEGETABLES

SERVES 6

This recipe is a variation of a wonderful dish invented by Sarah Leah Chase for her specialty food store in Nantucket, Que Sera Sarah. All these vegetables ripen at the same time and they're readily available, so you can make enough to feed a crowd. Add the dressing when the orzo is still warm so it absorbs into the pasta. This dish is even better made in advance; just check the seasonings and add the pine nuts, feta, and basil leaves at the last minute.

1	small eggplant, peeled and ¾-inch diced
1	red bell pepper, 1-inch diced
1	yellow bell pepper, 1-inch diced
1	red onion, peeled and 1-inch diced
2	garlic cloves, minced
⅓ cup	good olive oil
1½ teaspoons	kosher salt
½ teaspoon	freshly ground black pepper
½ pound	orzo

FOR THE DRESSING

⅓ cup	freshly squeezed lemon juice (2 lemons)
⅓ cup	good olive oil
1 teaspoon	kosher salt
½ teaspoon	freshly ground black pepper

TO ASSEMBLE

4	scallions, minced (white and green parts)
¼ cup	pignolis, toasted (see page 101)
¾ pound	good feta, ½-inch diced (not crumbled)
15	fresh basil leaves, cut into chiffonade

Preheat the oven to 425 degrees. Toss the eggplant, bell peppers, onion, and garlic with the olive oil, salt, and pepper on a large baking sheet. Roast for 40 minutes, until browned, turning once with a spatula.

Meanwhile, cook the orzo in boiling salted water for 7 to 9 minutes, until tender. Drain and transfer to a large serving bowl.

Add the roasted vegetables to the pasta, scraping all the liquid and seasonings from the roasting pan into the pasta bowl.

For the dressing, combine the lemon juice, olive oil, salt, and pepper and pour on the pasta and vegetables. Let cool to room temperature, then add the scallions, pignolis, feta, and basil. Check the seasonings, and serve at room temperature.

APPLE CROSTATA

SERVES 6

This is my absolute, all-time favorite dessert. I've made it so often that I'm sure my friends are saying behind my back, "No, not the apple crostata again," but there's never a crumb left. It's adapted from a recipe in Cucina Simpatica, *written by dear friends Johanne Killeen and George Germon, who own Al Forno restaurant in Providence, Rhode Island.*

FOR THE PASTRY (2 TARTS)

2 cups	all-purpose flour
¼ cup	granulated or superfine sugar
½ teaspoon	kosher salt
½ pound	very cold unsalted butter, diced

FOR THE FILLING (1 TART)

1½ pounds	McIntosh, Macoun, or Empire apples
¼ teaspoon	grated orange zest
¼ cup	all-purpose flour
¼ cup	granulated or superfine sugar
¼ teaspoon	kosher salt
¼ teaspoon	ground cinnamon
⅛ teaspoon	ground allspice
4 tablespoons	cold unsalted butter (½ stick), diced

For the pastry, place the flour, sugar, and salt in the bowl of a food processor fitted with a steel blade. Pulse a few times to combine. Add the butter and toss quickly with your fingers to coat each cube of butter with the flour. Be careful; the blades are sharp. Pulse 12 to 15 times, or until the butter is the size of peas. With the motor running, add ¼ cup ice water all at once through the feed tube. Keep hitting the pulse button to combine, but stop the machine just before the dough comes together. Turn the dough out onto a well-floured board and form into 2 disks. Wrap with plastic and refrigerate one of the disks for at least an hour. Freeze the rest of the pastry.

Preheat the oven to 450 degrees.

Roll the pastry into an 11-inch circle on a lightly floured surface. Transfer it to a baking sheet lined with parchment paper.

For the filling, peel, core, and quarter the apples. Cut each quarter into 3 chunks. Toss the chunks with the orange zest. Cover the tart dough with the apple chunks, leaving a 1½-inch border.

Combine the flour, sugar, salt, cinnamon, and allspice in the bowl of a food processor fitted with a steel blade. Add the butter and pulse until the mixture is crumbly. Pour into a bowl and rub it with your fingers until it starts holding together. Sprinkle evenly on the apples. Gently fold the border over the apples, pleating it to make a circle.

Bake the crostata for 20 to 25 minutes, or until the crust is golden and the apples are tender. Let the tart cool for 5 minutes, then use 2 large spatulas to transfer it to a wire rack.

A Party for Eight

Perfect Roast Turkey

Spinach Gratin

NOT THANKSGIVING

Smashed Sweet Potatoes with Apples

Popovers

Plum Tart

Vanilla Armagnac Ice Cream

SHAKE UP TRADITION

Last spring, I invited some very special friends to dinner. I wanted to make a meal that would surprise and delight them but wouldn't require me to spend a week in the kitchen. The guest of honor was an American writer living in Paris; he not only writes about food but is a wonderful cook himself. I thought, what could I make that would really please him?

Because he clearly eats French food all the time, I decided to make the most American dinner I could think of, and what's more American than roast turkey? But, I thought, it's not Thanksgiving—wouldn't that be odd? Then I decided, that's just it: It *is* odd, and it's just the kind of surprise that I like. It's delicious, and it's the last thing he would expect me to make, so it's *perfect*.

The real secret here is that roast turkey is one of the easiest meals I can make. I roasted it the way I roast a chicken, with the vegetables —fennel, carrots, onions, and potatoes—right in the pan. Then I made spinach gratin, smashed sweet potatoes, and popovers. When we were ready to sit down to dinner at the kitchen table, I had the plum tart cooling on the stove. Almost everything was made in advance, so I could spend all my time at the party. The atmosphere felt like sitting down with your family, and it was one of the most magical evenings I can remember.

The next week, my friend e-mailed me from Paris. He told me that he gave a "bite-by-bite" description of the meal to his wife, who unfortunately had not been able to join us. He said she was so annoyed and jealous that she made him sleep on the sofa that night. I guess the dinner was a success.

PERFECT
ROAST TURKEY
SERVES 8

Remember how your mother used to get up at 4 A.M. on Thanksgiving so she could put the turkey in the oven to roast for ten hours? Then she had to baste it all day to keep it from drying out, which, of course, it did anyway? Forget it. A 12- to 15-pound turkey cooks in 2 to 3 hours, and you let it rest for at least 20 minutes before you carve it. Everyone will say, "This is the best turkey I ever ate." I use an organic turkey whenever I can.

1	fresh turkey (12 pounds)
	Kosher salt
	Freshly ground black pepper
1	large bunch of fresh thyme
1	lemon, halved
3	Spanish onions
1 head	garlic, halved crosswise
4 tablespoons	butter (½ stick), melted
½ cup	good olive oil
8	carrots, peeled and cut into 2-inch chunks
10	red new potatoes, halved
3 heads	fennel, fronds removed, cut into wedges through the core

Preheat the oven to 350 degrees.

Take the giblets out of the turkey and wash the turkey inside and out. Remove any excess fat and leftover pinfeathers and pat the outside dry. Place the turkey in a large roasting pan. Liberally salt and pepper the inside of the turkey cavity. Stuff the cavity with the thyme, lemon, one of the onions (quartered), and the garlic. Brush the outside of the turkey with the butter and sprinkle with salt and pepper. Tie the legs together with string and tuck the wing tips under the body of the turkey. Peel and slice the remaining onions, toss them with ¼ cup olive oil, and scatter them around the turkey.

Roast the turkey for 1 hour. Toss the carrots, potatoes, and fennel with ¼ cup olive oil and add to the roasting pan. Continue to roast for about 1½ hours, or until the juices run clear when you cut between the leg and the thigh. Remove the turkey to a cutting board and cover with aluminum foil; let rest for 20 minutes.

Stir the vegetables and return the pan to the oven. Continue to cook the vegetables while the turkey rests. Slice the turkey and serve on a platter with the roasted vegetables.

SPINACH GRATIN

Fresh spinach is much more work and not much different in flavor in this dish. Use frozen.

Paul Hodges is a wonderful cook at Barefoot Contessa. He makes the best creamed spinach in the world. I decided to sprinkle it with grated cheese and bake it to make a gratin. It was creamy on the inside and browned and crunchy on the top. You can assemble the dish with the cheese topping a day or two ahead, then bake it before serving.

4 tablespoons	unsalted butter (½ stick)
4 cups	chopped yellow onions (2 large)
¼ cup	all-purpose flour
¼ teaspoon	grated nutmeg
1 cup	heavy cream
2 cups	milk
About 3 pounds	frozen chopped spinach, defrosted (5 10-ounce packages)
1 cup	freshly grated Parmesan cheese
1 tablespoon	kosher salt
½ teaspoon	freshly ground black pepper
½ cup	grated Gruyère cheese

Preheat the oven to 425 degrees.

Melt the butter in a heavy-bottomed sauté pan over medium heat. Add the onions and sauté until translucent, about 15 minutes. Add the flour and nutmeg and cook, stirring, for 2 more minutes. Add the cream and milk and cook until thickened.

Squeeze as much liquid as possible from the spinach and add the spinach to the sauce. Add ½ cup of the Parmesan cheese and mix well. Season to taste with the salt and pepper.

Transfer the spinach to a baking dish and sprinkle the remaining ½ cup Parmesan and the Gruyère on top. Bake for 20 minutes, or until hot and bubbly. Serve immediately.

SMASHED SWEET POTATOES WITH APPLES

SERVES 8

Parker Hodges, the chef at Barefoot Contessa, decided to substitute caramelized apples for the traditional marshmallows on the top of a sweet potato puree. I think it's delicious and adds a flavor that's more tart than sweet. You can always make two small dishes: one with apples for the adults and one with marshmallows for the kids. Both versions are always on the Barefoot Contessa holiday menu.

4 pounds	sweet potatoes (about 6 large)
½ cup	freshly squeezed orange juice
½ cup	heavy cream
4 tablespoons	unsalted butter (½ stick), melted
¼ cup	light brown sugar
1 teaspoon	ground nutmeg
½ teaspoon	ground cinnamon
2 teaspoons	kosher salt
1 teaspoon	freshly ground black pepper

FOR THE TOPPING

3 tablespoons	unsalted butter
3	McIntosh or Macoun apples, peeled, cored, and cut into eighths
3 tablespoons	light brown sugar

Preheat the oven to 375 degrees.

Scrub the potatoes, prick them several times with a knife or fork, and bake them for 1 hour, or until very soft when pierced with a knife. Remove from the oven and scoop out the insides as soon as they are cool enough to handle. Place the sweet potato meat into the bowl of an electric mixer fitted with the paddle attachment and add the

orange juice, cream, butter, brown sugar, nutmeg, cinnamon, salt, and pepper. Mix together until combined but not smooth, and pour into a baking dish.

For the topping, melt the butter in a skillet over medium-high heat. Add the apple wedges and brown sugar and cook for about 5 to 10 minutes, until lightly browned on both sides. Place on top of the sweet potatoes.

Bake the potatoes and apples for 20 to 30 minutes, until heated through.

It may be called a yam in the grocery, but chances are it's a sweet potato, which comes in many colors from pale yellow to dark orange (see pages 150–151).

POPOVERS

MAKES 12

There are three secrets to great popovers: Make sure the pan is hot before you pour in the batter, fill each section not more than half full, and no peeking while they're in the oven. They're much easier than you expect, and they make any meal feel festive.

1½ tablespoons	unsalted butter, melted, plus softened butter for greasing pans
1½ cups	all-purpose flour, sifted
¾ teaspoon	kosher salt
3	extra-large eggs at room temperature
1½ cups	whole milk at room temperature

Preheat the oven to 425 degrees.

Generously grease aluminum popover pans or custard cups with softened butter. You'll need enough pans to make 12 popovers. Place the pans in the oven for 2 minutes to preheat. Meanwhile, whisk together the flour, salt, eggs, milk, and melted butter until smooth. The batter will be thin. Fill the popover pans less than half full and bake for exactly 30 minutes. Do not peek.

Serve hot.

The easiest way to pour batter into the pans is with a liquid measuring cup.

PLUM TART

MAKES ONE 9 1/2 -INCH TART

I've made lots of plum tarts over the years because I love Italian prune plums, which are in season in late summer and early autumn. But my favorite plum tart comes from my dear friend Anna Pump, who has written many of the Loaves and Fishes cookbooks and has taught me more about food than anyone I know. This recipe is adapted from her Loaves and Fishes Party Cookbook. *Since I love the combination of prunes and Armagnac, I've made Vanilla Armagnac Ice Cream (recipe follows) to accompany this delicious tart.*

2 cups	all-purpose flour
¾ cup	finely chopped walnuts
¾ cup	light brown sugar, lightly packed
12 tablespoons	cold unsalted butter (1½ sticks), diced
1	egg yolk
2 pounds	firm, ripe Italian prune plums, pitted and quartered lengthwise

Use a metal measuring cup to make a straight edge.

Preheat the oven to 400 degrees.

Combine the flour, walnuts, and sugar in a large bowl. Add the butter and the egg yolk. Mix, either by hand or with an electric mixer, until crumbly.

Press 1½ cups of the crumb mixture in an even layer into the bottom of a 9½-inch springform or tart pan. Arrange the plums in the pan, skin-side down, to form a flower pattern; begin at the outside and work your way in.

Sprinkle the rest of the crumb mixture evenly over the plums. Bake the tart for 40 to 50 minutes, or until it's lightly browned and the plum juices are bubbling. Remove from the oven and cool for 10 minutes. Remove from the pan and transfer the tart to a flat plate. Serve warm or at room temperature.

VANILLA ARMAGNAC ICE CREAM

MAKES 1 QUART

Sometimes the easiest recipes are the best. This is based on the ice cream that was made for hundreds of years in Philadelphia. It's very rich but light. Rather than making a custard, all you do is flavor heavy cream, then freeze it in an ice cream freezer.

3 cups	heavy cream
⅔ cup	sugar
1 teaspoon	pure vanilla extract
	Seeds scraped from 1 vanilla bean
¼ cup	good Armagnac

Warm the cream, sugar, vanilla, and vanilla seeds in a small saucepan over medium heat until the sugar is dissolved. Be sure that all the sugar is dissolved; you will no longer feel any grittiness from the sugar when you rub some cream between your fingers. Strain into a bowl, cover, and chill well.

Add the Armagnac and freeze the mixture in an ice cream freezer according to the manufacturer's directions. Spoon into a freezer container and allow to chill in the freezer for a few hours before serving.

This is a soft ice cream, so there's no need to soften it before serving.

Armagnac is brandy from the Gascony region of France. You can use Cognac or good brandy instead.

A Party for Twenty-five

Herbed Goat Cheese Sandwiches

Cheddar and Chutney on Brioche

Lemon Bars

Lime Curd and Long-Stemmed Strawberries

Carrot Cake Cupcakes

AFTERNOON TEA

Orange Chocolate Chunk Cake

Fruit Tarts

Shortbread Cookies with Dragées

Chocolate Ganache Cake*

Champagne and Tea

*page 88

MY BEST PARTY

When my first book, *The Barefoot Contessa Cookbook,* was published in the summer of 1999, I felt like celebrating. My husband and I gave a garden party and invited everyone in my world: friends from East Hampton and New York, extraordinary people who had helped me with the book, everyone from Barefoot Contessa, wonderful customers from the store, and farmers who had brought us superb produce and poultry over the years. The weather was perfect—75 degrees and sunny—and the garden did its "thing" with uncanny timing. I wanted it to be a terrific party, and with 350 guests, I knew it had to be planned so that I had absolutely nothing to do except visit with people while the party was going on.

First, we set up a lemonade stand "manned" by three adorable boys to set the tone as summer and casual. Waiters greeted everyone with trays of glasses filled with delicious chilled rosé and Pellegrino. I set up two huge tables: One held savory things such as baked Virginia ham and crab cakes from my book; the second table was an English tea with smoked salmon tea sandwiches, raisin scones, and long-stemmed strawberries. I love to do enormous food tables that are the centerpiece of a party; not only do they look festive, but it means that I need only a few people to replenish the tables rather than a team of waiters passing appetizers on silver trays.

This party is like that summer party: an afternoon tea. It's an easy party to give during the holidays when everyone is running from house to house, but it's also fun any time of year. The good news is that the tea sandwiches are served at room temperature and the desserts can be prepared in advance and arranged on the table an hour before guests arrive. I hope you'll find that it's a successful formula for a party that you'll do over and over again.

HERBED GOAT CHEESE SANDWICHES

MAKES 40 TO 45 SANDWICHES

We've been making this goat cheese spread for years at Barefoot Contessa. When I thought of making cucumber tea sandwiches, I decided that this spread would be a good complement. The spread will keep for weeks in the refrigerator. Prepare these sandwiches early in the day and keep them covered with damp paper towels and plastic wrap in the refrigerator.

FOR THE SPREAD (MAKES 2 1/3 CUPS)

8 ounces	cream cheese at room temperature
10½ ounces	Montrachet or other mild goat cheese at room temperature
1½ teaspoons	minced garlic (2 cloves)
½ teaspoon	minced fresh thyme leaves
3 tablespoons	minced fresh parsley
5 to 6 tablespoons	milk, half-and-half, or heavy cream
¾ teaspoon	kosher salt
½ teaspoon	freshly ground black pepper

FOR THE SANDWICHES

2 loaves	7-grain bread, thinly sliced
1	hothouse cucumber, not peeled

For the spread, place the cream cheese, goat cheese, garlic, thyme, parsley, 5 tablespoons milk, salt, and pepper in the bowl of an electric mixer fitted with the paddle attachment. Beat on medium speed until well mixed. Add an additional tablespoon of milk if the spread is very thick.

To make the sandwiches, spread each slice of bread with the goat cheese spread. Slice the cucumber in thin rounds and arrange on half the bread slices. Top with the remaining bread. Press slightly, trim off the crusts, and cut the sandwiches into halves, thirds, or triangles.

CHEDDAR AND CHUTNEY ON BRIOCHE

MAKES 40 SANDWICHES

Cheddar and chutney are a classic English combination. On mini brioche rolls from Eli's Bread, they're even better, but you can use any good bread.

40	mini brioche rolls
1 to 2 jars	Major Grey's chutney
1½ pounds	very good extra-sharp cheddar

Cut each roll in half crosswise. Spread the bottom half liberally with chutney. Place a thick slice of cheddar on top and cover with the top half of the roll.

I like English farmhouse cheddar, but any aged cheddar from Vermont will be delicious.

LEMON BARS

It's important to me that lemon bars really taste like lemon. I love the way the tart citrus cuts the sweetness of the filling. I can't begin to calculate how many lemon bars Harry Goodale has made at Barefoot Contessa over the years, but they're definitely one of our best sellers.

FOR THE CRUST

½ pound	unsalted butter at room temperature
½ cup	granulated sugar
2 cups	all-purpose flour
⅛ teaspoon	kosher salt

FOR THE FILLING

6	extra-large eggs at room temperature
3 cups	granulated sugar
2 tablespoons	grated lemon zest (4 to 6 lemons)
1 cup	freshly squeezed lemon juice
1 cup	all-purpose flour

Confectioners' sugar, for dusting

Preheat the oven to 350 degrees.

For the crust, cream the butter and sugar until light in the bowl of an electric mixer fitted with the paddle attachment. Combine the flour and salt and, with the mixer on low, add to the butter until just mixed. Dump the dough onto a well-floured board and gather into a ball. Flatten the dough with floured hands and press it into a 9 × 13 × 2-inch baking sheet, building up a ½-inch edge on all sides. Chill.

Bake the crust for 15 to 20 minutes, until very lightly browned. Let cool on a wire rack. Leave the oven on.

For the filling, whisk together the eggs, sugar, lemon zest, lemon juice, and flour. Pour over the crust and bake for 30 to 35 minutes, until the filling is set. Let cool to room temperature.

Cut into triangles and dust with confectioners' sugar.

LIME CURD

MAKES 3 CUPS

I like lime curd with character, and for me that means lots of zest. Lime curd is wonderful on a slice of toast, as a dip for long-stemmed straw-berries, or as a sauce with pound cake and fresh fruit. It lasts for weeks in the refrigerator.

4	limes at room temperature
1½ cups	sugar
¼ pound	unsalted butter at room temperature
4	extra-large eggs at room temperature
⅛ teaspoon	kosher salt

Remove the zest from the limes with a carrot peeler, being careful to avoid the white pith. Put the zest in the bowl of a food processor fit-ted with a steel blade. Add the sugar and pulse until the zest is very finely minced. Squeeze the limes and measure out ½ cup juice.

Cream the butter in the bowl of an electric mixer fitted with a pad-dle attachment, then beat in the sugar and lime zest. Add the eggs, one at a time, then add the lime juice and salt. Mix until combined.

Pour the mixture into a 2-quart saucepan and cook over low heat until thickened, about 10 minutes, stirring constantly. The lime curd will be ready when it coats a spoon, and it will register about 175 degrees on a candy thermometer. Be careful not to overcook, or it will curdle. Remove from the heat and let cool or refrigerate.

For lemon or orange curd, substitute equal measures of lemon or orange for lime in this recipe.

CARROT CAKE CUPCAKES

MAKES 22 CUPCAKES

The carrot cake at Barefoot Contessa used to be very dense and rich. A few years ago I decided to update it, and it was an immediate hit. This is moist and light and, of course, the perfect vehicle for all that thick, creamy frosting.

2 cups	granulated sugar
1⅓ cups	vegetable oil
3	extra-large eggs at room temperature
1 teaspoon	pure vanilla extract
2 cups	all-purpose flour plus 1 tablespoon
2 teaspoons	ground cinnamon
2 teaspoons	baking soda
1½ teaspoons	kosher salt
1 pound	carrots, grated
1 cup	raisins
1 cup	chopped walnuts

FOR THE FROSTING

¾ pound	cream cheese at room temperature
½ pound	unsalted butter at room temperature
1 teaspoon	pure vanilla extract
1 pound	confectioners' sugar, sieved

FOR THE DECORATION

2 tablespoons	unsalted butter
1 cup	grated or shaved carrots
3 tablespoons	good maple syrup

Preheat the oven to 400 degrees. Line muffin pans with paper liners.

Beat the sugar, oil, and eggs together in the bowl of an electric mixer fitted with the paddle attachment until light yellow. Add the vanilla. In another bowl, sift together 2 cups flour, the cinnamon, baking soda, and salt.

Add the dry ingredients to the wet ingredients. Toss the carrots, raisins, and walnuts with 1 tablespoon flour. Add to the batter and mix well (I use my hands—it works best!).

Scoop the batter into the muffin cups until each is almost full. Bake for 10 minutes, then lower the oven to 350 degrees and bake for 35 minutes, or until a toothpick comes out clean. Let cool on a wire rack.

For the frosting, mix the cream cheese, butter, and vanilla in the bowl of an electric mixer fitted with the paddle attachment until *just* combined. Add the sugar and mix until smooth.

For the decoration, melt the butter in a skillet over medium heat; add the carrots and maple syrup and sauté for 2 to 3 minutes, until the carrots are tender. Spread them on a paper towel to cool.

When the cupcakes are cool, frost them generously and garnish with big pinches of sautéed carrots.

ORANGE CHOCOLATE CHUNK CAKE

MAKES ONE 10-INCH BUNDT CAKE

For years, Barefoot Contessa has been making a wonderful orange pound cake that is moist and flavorful. When my friend Anna Pump at Loaves and Fishes added chocolate chunks to her orange cake, I thought it was such a good idea that I borrowed it and added chocolate chunks to ours. The combination of tart, citrusy orange with sweet chocolate has been a big hit.

½ pound	unsalted butter at room temperature
2 cups	sugar
4	extra-large eggs at room temperature
¼ cup	grated orange zest (4 large oranges)
3 cups	all-purpose flour plus 2 tablespoons
½ teaspoon	baking powder
½ teaspoon	baking soda
1 teaspoon	kosher salt
¼ cup	freshly squeezed orange juice
¾ cup	buttermilk at room temperature
1 teaspoon	pure vanilla extract
2 cups	good semisweet chocolate chunks

FOR THE SYRUP

¼ cup	sugar
¼ cup	freshly squeezed orange juice

FOR THE GANACHE

8 ounces	good semisweet chocolate chips
½ cup	heavy cream
1 teaspoon	instant coffee granules

Preheat the oven to 350 degrees. Grease and flour a 10-inch Bundt pan.

Cream the butter and sugar in the bowl of an electric mixer fitted with the paddle attachment for about 5 minutes, or until light and fluffy. Add the eggs, one at a time, then the orange zest.

Sift together 3 cups flour, the baking powder, baking soda, and salt in a large bowl. In another bowl, combine the orange juice, buttermilk, and vanilla. Add the flour and buttermilk mixtures alternately in thirds to the creamed butter, beginning and ending with the flour. Toss the chocolate chunks with 2 tablespoons flour and add to the batter. Pour into the pan, smooth the top, and bake for 45 minutes to 1 hour, until a cake tester comes out clean. Let the cake cool in the pan on a wire rack for 10 minutes.

Meanwhile, make the syrup. In a small saucepan over medium-low heat, cook the sugar with the orange juice until the sugar dissolves. Remove the cake from the pan, set it on a rack over a tray, and spoon the orange syrup over the cake. Allow the cake to cool completely.

For the ganache, melt the chocolate, heavy cream, and coffee in the top of a double boiler over simmering water until smooth and warm, stirring occasionally. Drizzle over the top of the cake.

FRUIT TARTS

MAKES SIXTEEN 3¾-INCH TARTS

Making piecrust can be daunting, but there are a few key steps that make all the difference. The goal is to have bits of butter visible in the dough, which will make the pastry flaky. First, freeze the flour and sugar for 30 minutes before starting. Second, use as little water as possible when mixing the dough. And finally, let the dough rest in the refrigerator for at least 30 minutes before rolling it out. This technique takes a bit of practice, but once you've mastered it, you'll never make bad pastry again.

FOR THE PASTRY

2½ cups	all-purpose flour
6 tablespoons	sugar
1 teaspoon	kosher salt
½ pound	very cold unsalted butter
6 to 8 tablespoons	ice water

FOR THE FILLING

1 cup	good raspberry jelly or preserves
	Small soft fruits such as grapes, berries, or sliced kiwis
½ cup	apricot preserves

I like the Raspberry Red Currant jelly made by Hero.

You can get 3¾-inch tart pans from Bridge Kitchenware in New York City.

Combine the flour, sugar, and salt; freeze it for 30 minutes. Dice the butter into medium pieces. Put the flour mixture in the bowl of a food processor fitted with a steel blade. Add the butter and pulse about 10 times, or until the butter is in small bits. Add the ice water and process until the dough comes together. Dump on a well-floured board and form into 2 disks. Wrap in plastic and chill for at least 30 minutes.

Preheat the oven to 375 degrees.

Roll out one of the disks of dough 1/16 inch thick, and cut circles large enough to fit the tart pans. It is important not to stretch the dough when placing it in the pans; be sure the circles are larger than the pans. Cut off the excess dough with a sharp knife or your thumb. Repeat with the remaining dough.

Line each tart shell with a piece of aluminum foil, and fill the shell with dried beans or rice. Bake for 10 minutes. Remove the foil and beans and prick the bottom of each shell with a fork in order to allow the steam to escape. Bake for another 8 to 10 minutes, until browned. Let cool to room temperature.

For the filling, place 1 tablespoon raspberry jelly in each cooled tart shell and arrange the fruit on top. Combine the apricot preserves with a few tablespoons of water in a small saucepan and heat until smooth and runny. Brush the top of the fruit with the glaze. Serve as soon as possible after filling so the pastry doesn't get soggy.

SHORTBREAD COOKIES WITH DRAGÉES

MAKES 24 COOKIES

This shortbread cookie recipe comes from Eli Zabar of E.A.T., the Vinegar Factory, Eli's Bread, and Eli's Manhattan in New York City. They are the quintessence of shortbread and have been my all-time favorite cookie since the first time I tried one more than fifteen years ago. Dragées give them a festive sparkle.

¾ pound	unsalted butter at room temperature
1 cup	granulated sugar
1 teaspoon	pure vanilla extract
3½ cups	all-purpose flour
¼ teaspoon	salt
1 cup	confectioners' sugar
	Silver dragées

The edges of the shortbread will be ever so slightly sharper if you chill the cookies for 10 minutes before you bake them.

You can mail-order dragées from Dean & Deluca or New York Cake and Baking Distributors.

Mix together the butter and granulated sugar in the bowl of an electric mixer fitted with the paddle attachment until just combined. Add the vanilla. In another bowl, sift together the flour and salt; add it to the butter and sugar. Mix until the dough starts to come together. Dump on a floured board and shape into a flat disk. Wrap in plastic and chill for 30 minutes.

Preheat the oven to 350 degrees.

Roll the dough ½ inch thick and cut with a 3-inch-round fluted cutter. Place on an ungreased baking sheet and bake for 20 to 25 minutes, until the edges begin to brown. Let cool to room temperature.

Combine the confectioners' sugar with about 2 tablespoons of water to make a very thin glaze. Spoon onto the cookies and sprinkle with a few dragées before the glaze dries.

WINTER PARTIES

A Party for Twenty

Seafood Chowder

Butternut Squash and Apple Soup

Fennel Soup Gratin

NEW YEAR'S DAY

Baked Virginia Ham

Cranberry Fruit Conserve

Green Salad

Old-Fashioned Apple Crisp

Vanilla Ice Cream

THAT'S ENTERTAINMENT!

I invite friends for lunch every year for New Year's Day. Entertaining on New Year's Day doesn't have any of the pressure of New Year's Eve, and we always have a terrific time. We each have the assignment to bring two of our favorite scenes from films. We rent videos and fast-forward them to the beginning of the scenes we love, then we all spend a lazy afternoon in front of the television watching movies. It's one of my favorite parties of the year.

For a party like this, I serve the kind of relaxed food you would have for an open house, so when people arrive they can help themselves from the buffet in the kitchen, then join us in the study to watch movies. Two large stockpots filled with soup are simmering on the stove: seafood chowder and butternut squash and apple soup, plus a rich fennel soup gratin warming in the oven. I put out a buffet of wonderful room-temperature things to eat, such as baked Virginia ham, cranberry fruit conserve, a big tossed green salad, and a wooden board with farmhouse Cheddar, English Stilton, and fresh breads. Dessert is a warm old-fashioned apple crisp with vanilla ice cream.

All year, I keep a running list of the scenes I want to watch. Some are funny, such as the scene from *The Graduate* when Mrs. Robinson tries to seduce Dustin Hoffman; some are harrowing, like the scene on the train from *Julia* when the Nazis check Lillian Hellman's passport; and some are charming, like Tom Cruise playing "air guitar" in *Risky Business* after his parents leave town. The fireplace is glowing, friends are arriving, and because absolutely everything can be done before the guests arrive, I'm as relaxed as I would be at someone else's party. I cherish this afternoon every year, and I hope you love making this party for *your* friends, too.

SEAFOOD
CHOWDER
MAKES 3 QUARTS

Parker and Paul Hodges make this soup at Barefoot Contessa. It takes longer than most of our recipes, but it is really worth it. It's hearty enough to serve alone as lunch or for dinner with bread and a salad.

This recipe can easily be doubled.

1 pound	large shrimp (32 to 36 per pound), peeled and deveined (save shells for stock)
½ pound	scallops
½ pound	monkfish
½ pound	fresh lump crabmeat, picked over to remove shells
¼ pound	unsalted butter
1 cup	peeled and medium-diced carrots (4 carrots)
½ cup	medium-diced yellow onion (1 onion)
1 cup	medium-diced celery (3 stalks)
1 cup	medium-diced small white or red potatoes
½ cup	corn kernels, fresh or frozen
¼ cup	all-purpose flour
1 recipe	Seafood Stock (recipe follows)
1½ tablespoons	heavy cream (optional)
2 tablespoons	minced parsley
	Salt and freshly ground black pepper to taste

Clam juice won't work as a substitute for the stock here, but your fish store may sell a good seafood stock that will.

Cut the shrimp, scallops, and monkfish into bite-sized pieces and place them in a bowl with the crabmeat.

In a heavy-bottomed pot, melt the butter; add the carrots, onions, celery, potatoes, and corn and sauté over medium-low heat for 15 minutes, or until the potatoes are barely cooked, stirring occasionally. Add the flour; reduce the heat to low and cook, stirring often, for 3 minutes. Add the Seafood Stock and bring to a boil. Add the seafood; reduce the heat and simmer, uncovered, for 7 to 10 minutes, until the fish is just cooked. Add the heavy cream, if desired, and the parsley. Add salt and pepper to taste, and serve.

SEAFOOD STOCK
MAKES ABOUT 1 QUART

You can make this stock in advance; it freezes beautifully.

2 tablespoons	good olive oil
	Shells from 1 pound large shrimp
2 cups	chopped yellow onions (2 onions)
2	carrots, unpeeled and chopped
3 stalks	celery, chopped
2	garlic cloves, minced
½ cup	good white wine
⅓ cup	tomato paste
1 tablespoon	kosher salt
1½ teaspoons	freshly ground black pepper
10	sprigs fresh thyme, including stems

Warm the oil in a stockpot over medium heat. Add the shrimp shells, onions, carrots, and celery and sauté for 15 minutes, or until lightly browned. Add the garlic and cook 2 more minutes. Add 1½ quarts of water, the white wine, tomato paste, salt, pepper, and thyme. Bring to a boil, then reduce the heat and simmer for 1 hour. Strain through a sieve, pressing the solids. You should have approximately 1 quart of stock. You can make up the difference with water or wine if you need to.

BUTTERNUT SQUASH AND APPLE SOUP
MAKES 3 1/2 QUARTS

This is my all-time favorite soup, and it's good for you. It's a vegetarian variation of a popular soup from The Silver Palate Cookbook *and is one of the best-selling soups at Barefoot Contessa. The creamy butternut squash and sweet apples balance the spicy curry.*

2 tablespoons	unsalted butter
2 tablespoons	good olive oil
4 cups	chopped yellow onions (3 large)
2 tablespoons	mild curry powder
5 pounds	butternut squash (2 large)
1½ pounds	sweet apples, such as McIntosh (4 apples)
2 teaspoons	kosher salt
½ teaspoon	freshly ground black pepper
2 cups	good apple juice or cider

Warm the butter and olive oil in a large stockpot over low heat. Add the onions and curry powder and cook, uncovered, for 15 to 20 minutes, until the onions are tender. Stir occasionally, scraping the bottom of the pot.

Peel the squash, cut in half, and remove the seeds. Cut the squash into chunks. Peel, quarter, and core the apples. Cut into chunks.

Add the squash, apples, salt, pepper, and 2 cups of water to the pot. Bring to a boil, then cover, reduce the heat to low, and cook for 30 to 40 minutes, until the squash and apples are very soft. Process the soup through a food mill fitted with a large blade, or puree it coarsely in the bowl of a food processor fitted with a steel blade.

Pour the soup back into the pot. Add the apple juice and enough water to make the soup the consistency you like; it should be slightly sweet and quite thick. Check the salt and pepper and serve hot.

FENNEL SOUP GRATIN

I love French onion soup with its deliciously gooey topping of melted cheese, and I also love the flavor of sautéed fennel, so I tried them together. It turned out to better than I expected. I gave the flavor a little extra help with a splash of Pernod at the end. This soup is also good as a winter lunch with a big green salad and fresh fruit for dessert.

¼ pound	unsalted butter
8 cups	thinly sliced fennel (2 large bulbs)
8 cups	thinly sliced yellow onions (4 large onions)
1½ teaspoons	minced fresh thyme leaves
¼ cup	brandy
½ cup	medium-dry sherry
½ cup	good white wine
8 cups	good chicken stock
1 tablespoon	kosher salt
1 teaspoon	freshly ground black pepper
¼ cup	Pernod
16 slices	crusty French bread
¾ pound	Gruyère cheese, grated

Pernod is anise-flavored liqueur from France.

Melt the butter in a large stockpot over medium-high heat. Add the fennel, onions, and thyme and sauté for 20 to 25 minutes, until the onions and fennel are very tender and caramelized. (You can add a little water if it starts to stick.) Deglaze the pan by adding the brandy; reduce the heat to medium and cook for 3 minutes, scraping the bottom of the pan. Add the sherry and white wine and simmer, uncovered, for 10 minutes. Add the chicken stock, salt, and pepper and continue to cook, uncovered, for another 15 minutes. Add the Pernod and cook for 5 more minutes. Check for salt and pepper.

Preheat the broiler.

Ladle the soup into 6 to 8 ovenproof bowls and place 1 or 2 slices of
French bread and a handful of Gruyère cheese on top of each bowl.
Place the bowls on a baking sheet and slide them under the broiler
for 3 minutes, or until the cheese is brown and bubbly, and serve.

BAKED VIRGINIA HAM

SERVES 20, WITH LEFTOVERS

This is so good and so easy! I included this recipe in my first book, but it's such a party staple for me that I had to make sure you had it handy for this buffet. Use leftovers to make ham and chutney sandwiches. Choose the best-quality smoked ham you can find; buy a spiral-cut ham or have the butcher slice and retie a whole ham.

1	fully cooked spiral-cut smoked ham (14 to 16 pounds)
6	garlic cloves, peeled
¾ cup	good mango chutney (8½ ounces)
½ cup	Dijon mustard
1 cup	light brown sugar, packed
	Zest of 1 orange
¼ cup	freshly squeezed orange juice

Shelburne Farms in Shelburne, Vermont, sells a delicious spiral-cut ham.

I use Major Grey's chutney.

Preheat the oven to 350 degrees.

Place the ham on a heavy roasting pan.

Mince the garlic in the bowl of a food processor fitted with a steel blade. Add the chutney, mustard, brown sugar, orange zest, and orange juice and process until smooth. Pour the glaze over the ham and bake for 1 hour, or until the ham is fully heated and the glaze is well browned. Serve hot or at room temperature.

CRANBERRY FRUIT CONSERVE

MAKES 4 CUPS

This is a variation of my favorite Craig Claiborne recipe from The New York Times Cookbook. *I've been making it since I was married in 1968. For the holidays at Barefoot Contessa, we offer it with or without nuts, and almost everyone orders it. It's great in turkey sandwiches all winter long.*

1	12-ounce bag of fresh cranberries, cleaned
1¾ cups	sugar
1	Granny Smith apple, peeled, cored, and chopped
	Grated zest and juice of 1 orange
	Grated zest and juice of 1 lemon
¾ cup	raisins
¾ cup	chopped walnuts or pecans

An excellent zester called a rasp makes zesting a breeze. It's available from Martha by Mail.

Cook the cranberries, sugar, and 1 cup of water in a saucepan over low heat for about 5 minutes, or until the skins pop open. Add the apple, zests, and juices and cook for 15 more minutes. Remove from the heat and add the raisins and nuts. Let cool, and serve chilled.

OLD-FASHIONED APPLE CRISP

SERVES 10

The oatmeal in the crust gives this crisp a homey texture. I assemble this early in the day and put it in the oven just before everyone arrives so the house smells wonderful all through the party. Make two for a crowd.

5 pounds	McIntosh or Macoun apples
	Grated zest of 1 orange
	Grated zest of 1 lemon
2 tablespoons	freshly squeezed orange juice
2 tablespoons	freshly squeezed lemon juice
½ cup	granulated sugar
2 teaspoons	ground cinnamon
1 teaspoon	ground nutmeg
	FOR THE TOPPING
1½ cups	all-purpose flour
¾ cup	granulated sugar
¾ cup	light brown sugar, packed
½ teaspoon	kosher salt
1 cup	oatmeal
½ pound	cold unsalted butter, diced

Preheat the oven to 350 degrees. Butter a 9 × 14 × 2-inch oval baking dish.

Peel, core, and cut the apples into large wedges. Combine the apples with the zests, juices, sugar, and spices. Pour into the dish.

To make the topping, combine the flour, sugars, salt, oatmeal, and cold butter in the bowl of an electric mixer fitted with the paddle attachment. Mix on low speed until the mixture is crumbly and the butter is the size of peas. Scatter evenly over the apples.

Place the crisp on a sheet pan and bake for one hour until the top is brown and the apples are bubbly. Serve warm.

A Party for Twelve

Chicken Chili

Corn Chips

Grated Cheddar

Sour Cream

Chopped Onion

SNOW DAY

Green Salad Vinaigrette

Chocolate Chunk Cookies

Peanut Butter Chocolate Chunk Cookies

Chocolate White Chocolate Chunk Cookies

Vanilla Ice Cream

Hot Mulled Cider

NOT JUST SATURDAY NIGHT

Where did we get the idea that Saturday night is the only time to invite friends to dinner? I suppose that because our parents did it, we never questioned the idea. When my husband and I lived in Washington, D.C., in the 1970s and I was giving lots of parties, I almost always held a dinner party on Saturday night. I loved getting ready for the parties, but the parties themselves were b-o-r-i-n-g. People are tired from a long week. The meal is more complicated—appetizers, first course, dinner, and dessert—than any other meal. And people are expected to stay for hours.

Every once in a while I'd invite guests for brunch on Sunday morning. We'd sit around on the carpeted platforms (remember those?) and I'd put out a buffet of smoked salmon, bagels, scrambled eggs, and hot croissants. We always had a fabulous time. Many years later when I was a caterer, I thought back to what worked for me and what didn't, and I realized that I needed to let go of the idea of entertaining on Saturday night.

Now I'm much more likely to entertain any other time of the week. When I invite my friends for lunch on Sunday, I serve a big pot of chicken chili with a green salad, grated English Cheddar, and a simple dessert such as chocolate white chocolate chunk cookies and vanilla ice cream. People are rested from a day off on Saturday, and they have more energy during the day than at night. Everyone comes for lunch around noon, and they're off to do something else by 3 o'clock. I've spent a wonderful afternoon with my friends, and the whole thing wasn't nearly as daunting as making dinner on Saturday night.

CHICKEN CHILI

SERVES 12

We had been making traditional chili at Barefoot Contessa for almost 20 years. I decided to update it with chicken to make it lighter, and it's even more popular than our regular chili.

8 cups	chopped yellow onions (6 onions)
¼ cup	good olive oil, plus extra for chicken
¼ cup	minced garlic (8 cloves)
4	red bell peppers, cored, seeded, and large-diced
4	yellow bell peppers, cored, seeded, and large-diced
2 teaspoons	chili powder
2 teaspoons	ground cumin
½ teaspoon	dried red pepper flakes, or to taste
½ teaspoon	cayenne pepper, or to taste
4 teaspoons	kosher salt, plus more for chicken
4	28-ounce cans whole peeled plum tomatoes in puree, undrained
½ cup	minced fresh basil leaves
8	split chicken breasts, bone in, skin on
	Freshly ground black pepper

FOR SERVING

Chopped onions, corn chips, grated cheddar, sour cream

Cook the onions in the oil over medium-low heat for 10 to 15 minutes, until translucent. Add the garlic and cook for 1 more minute. Add the bell peppers, chili powder, cumin, red pepper flakes, cayenne, and salt. Cook for 1 minute. Crush the tomatoes by hand or in batches in a food processor fitted with a steel blade (pulse 6 to 8 times). Add to the pot with the basil. Bring to a boil, then reduce the heat and simmer, uncovered, for 30 minutes, stirring occasionally.

Preheat the oven to 350 degrees.

Rub the chicken breasts with olive oil and place them on a baking sheet. Sprinkle generously with salt and pepper. Roast the chicken for 35 to 40 minutes, until just cooked. Let cool slightly. Separate the meat from the bones and skin and cut it into ¾-inch chunks. Add to the chili and simmer, uncovered, for another 20 minutes. Serve with the toppings, or refrigerate and reheat gently before serving.

CHOCOLATE CHUNK COOKIES

MAKES 36 TO 40 COOKIES

These cookies are so good. They're crisp on the outside and creamy on the inside, and the chocolate chunks make them just so gooey. Be sure to use chocolate chunks, because chocolate chips don't have enough chocolate flavor. It's important to underbake the cookies to get the right texture.

½ pound	unsalted butter at room temperature
1 cup	light brown sugar, packed
½ cup	granulated sugar
2 teaspoons	pure vanilla extract
2	extra-large eggs at room temperature
2 cups	all-purpose flour
1 teaspoon	baking soda
1 teaspoon	kosher salt
1½ cups	chopped walnuts
1¼ pounds	semisweet chocolate chunks

Preheat the oven to 350 degrees.

Cream the butter and two sugars until light and fluffy in the bowl of an electric mixer fitted with the paddle attachment. Add the vanilla, then the eggs, one at a time, and mix well. Sift together the flour, baking soda, and salt and add to the butter with the mixer on low speed, mixing only until combined. Fold in the walnuts and chocolate chunks.

Nestlé makes chocolate chunks that are perfect for this recipe.

Drop the dough on a baking sheet lined with parchment paper, using a 1¾-inch-diameter ice cream scoop or a rounded tablespoon. Dampen your hands and flatten the dough slightly. Bake for exactly 15 minutes (the cookies will seem underdone). Remove from the oven and let cool slightly on the pan, then transfer to a wire rack to cool completely.

PEANUT BUTTER CHOCOLATE CHUNK COOKIES

MAKES 36 TO 40 COOKIES

This is my favorite variation of the old Barefoot Contessa chocolate chunk cookie recipe. It has the combination of flavors in a Reese's Peanut Butter Cup. Yum!

½ pound	unsalted butter at room temperature
1½ cups	light brown sugar, packed
¾ cup	granulated sugar
2	extra-large eggs at room temperature
2 teaspoons	pure vanilla extract
1 cup	good smooth peanut butter
2½ cups	all-purpose flour
1 teaspoon	baking powder
1 teaspoon	kosher salt
1 pound	good semisweet chocolate chunks

Preheat the oven to 350 degrees.

In the bowl of an electric mixer fitted with the paddle attachment, cream the butter and sugars until light and fluffy. Add the eggs, one at a time. Add the vanilla and peanut butter, and mix. Sift together the flour, baking powder, and salt and add to the batter, mixing only until combined. Fold in the chocolate chunks.

Drop the dough on a baking sheet lined with parchment paper, using either a 1¾-inch ice cream scoop or a rounded tablespoon. Dampen your hands, flatten the dough lightly, then press the tines of a wet fork in both directions. Bake for exactly 17 minutes (the cookies will seem underdone). Do not overbake. Remove from the oven and let cool slightly on the pan, then transfer to a wire rack and let cool completely.

CHOCOLATE WHITE CHOCOLATE CHUNK COOKIES

MAKES 40 TO 48 COOKIES

These are "reverse" chocolate chunk cookies; chocolate dough with white chocolate chunks. I prefer white chocolate to traditional chocolate, so I think these are wonderful.

½ pound	unsalted butter at room temperature
1 cup	light brown sugar, packed
1 cup	granulated sugar
2 teaspoons	pure vanilla extract
2	extra-large eggs at room temperature
⅔ cup	good unsweetened cocoa
2 cups	all-purpose flour
1 teaspoon	baking soda
1 teaspoon	kosher salt
1½ pounds	good white chocolate, coarsely chopped

I like Pernigotti cocoa powder from Williams-Sonoma.

Preheat the oven to 350 degrees.

Cream the butter and two sugars until light and fluffy in the bowl of an electric mixer fitted with the paddle attachment. Add the vanilla, then the eggs, one at a time, and mix well. Add the cocoa and mix again. Sift together the flour, baking soda, and salt and add to the chocolate with the mixer on low speed until just combined. Fold in the chopped white chocolate.

Drop the dough on a baking sheet lined with parchment paper, using a 1¾-inch ice cream scoop or a rounded tablespoon. Dampen your hands and flatten the dough slightly. Bake for exactly 15 minutes (the cookies will seem underdone). Remove from the oven and let cool slightly on the pan, then transfer to a wire rack to cool completely.

HOT MULLED
CIDER
SERVES 12

Nothing tastes as good on a cold winter day as hot spiced cider. It's easy to make and really warms your insides after an afternoon of winter sports. And nothing makes a house smell as wonderful. For a party, I leave it on the stove over very low heat and everyone helps themselves.

16 cups	apple cider or pure apple juice
4	2-inch cinnamon sticks
	Zest and juice of 2 oranges
8	whole cloves
6	star anise

Combine all the ingredients in a large saucepan and simmer over low heat for 5 to 10 minutes. Pour into mugs and serve.

Commercially prepared mulling spices, which combine many of these ingredients, can be added to the apple cider to make preparation even easier.

A Party for Six

Cheese Straws

Black Olives

VALENTINE'S DINNER

Roast Loin of Pork with Fennel

Sautéed Cabbage

Pears, English Stilton, and Port

ASSEMBLING MEALS

Despite all the time I have spent cooking at Barefoot Contessa, at home I think of myself as someone who assembles rather than cooks. I love to shop for delicious ingredients and serve them as is, rather than spending the day cooking and baking. I sometimes think about the afternoon that my friend Frank Newbold and I spent on an extraordinary terrace in the hills overlooking the beautiful harbor of Portofino, Italy. We sat in the warm October sun and watched the sailboats in the water below. Cocktails were served with three perfect little glazed Italian bowls of potato chips, pistachios, and oil-cured olives. I was in heaven.

For years I served the same appetizers with Campari and soda. My friends were delighted to have an elegant excuse to eat potato chips, and they loved the pistachios and olives. Why would I want to spend hours at the stove making hors d'oeuvres when my guests enjoyed such simple treats? No matter how much I love to cook, I also love to enjoy my own parties, and having less to do before guests arrive is important to me. I also know that serving truly simple ingredients makes everyone stop and really taste, such as the sweetness of a ripe red Bartlett pear and the sharpness of a good English Stilton when they're served as is. After a Chinese dinner, thin slices of a perfectly ripe Galia melon or, for the moment they are in season, fresh lychees served on ice are more special than the richest, most labor-intensive dessert.

Assembled appetizers, clockwise from top left: Galia melon and prosciutto, Macy's cheesesticks, olives, and Eli's potato chips.

Valentine's Day is traditionally spent with the one person you love, but I like to extend it to a few *friends* who I really love. I didn't have lots of time one year, so I decided to see how much of the meal I could assemble rather than cook. After dinner everyone clapped, which certainly confirmed my belief that, in fact, the *less* I do, the more fun the party can be.

ROAST LOIN OF PORK WITH FENNEL

SERVES 6

I didn't grow up eating pork, so I was pleased to find out how lean and flavorful it was when I made this roast loin of pork. I cooked it the way I cook lots of meats—roasted with carrots, potatoes, and fennel. It's important to let meat rest after it's cooked; you'll find that all meats become juicier and more tender after 15 to 20 minutes. The rub on this comes from my dear friend Anna Pump and her wonderful Loaves and Fishes Cookbook.

2	garlic cloves, minced
1 tablespoon	kosher salt
1 tablespoon	fresh thyme leaves
¼ cup	Dijon mustard
1	3-pound boneless pork loin, trimmed and tied
3	small fennel bulbs, tops removed
10	carrots, peeled and thickly sliced diagonally
10	small potatoes, quartered
2	onions, thickly sliced
4 tablespoons	good olive oil
4 tablespoons	unsalted butter (½ stick), melted
	Salt and freshly ground black pepper

Preheat the oven to 425 degrees.

With a mortar and pestle or in the bowl of a food processor fitted with a steel blade, grind together the garlic, salt, and thyme leaves. Add the mustard and combine. Spread the mixture over the loin of pork and allow it to sit at room temperature for at least 30 minutes.

Meanwhile, cut the fennel bulbs into thick wedges, slicing through the core. Toss the fennel, carrots, potatoes, and onions in a bowl with the olive oil, melted butter, salt, and pepper.

Transfer the vegetables to a large roasting pan and cook for 30 minutes. Add the pork loin to the pan and continue to cook for another 30 to 50 minutes, or until a meat thermometer inserted into the middle of the pork reads exactly 138 degrees. Remove the meat from the pan and return the vegetables to the oven to keep cooking. Cover the meat with aluminum foil and allow it to rest for 15 minutes.

Remove the strings from the meat and slice it thickly. Arrange the meat and vegetables on a platter. Sprinkle with salt and pepper.

SAUTÉED CABBAGE

SERVES 6

Martha Stewart taught me this dish and it is the essence of her cooking. The cabbage she used came from her garden in Maine, but of course you can buy it anywhere. The cabbage takes a minute to slice and fifteen minutes to cook, and it's so delicious that you can't stop eating it. Martha served it in summer with steamed lobster, but I love to serve it in winter with roast loin of pork.

1	small head of white cabbage, including outer green leaves (2½ pounds)
2 tablespoons	unsalted butter
1½ teaspoons	kosher salt
½ teaspoon	freshly ground black pepper
	Fleur de sel to taste (optional)

Fleur de sel is French sea salt.

Cut the cabbage in half and, with the cut-side down, slice it as thinly as possible around the core, as though you were making coleslaw. Discard the core.

Melt the butter in a large sauté pan or heavy-bottomed pot over medium-high heat. Add the cabbage, kosher salt, and pepper and sauté for 10 to 15 minutes, stirring occasionally, until the cabbage is tender and begins to brown. Finish with another sprinkling of kosher salt or fleur de sel. Serve hot.

PEARS,
ENGLISH STILTON,
AND PORT

My favorite winter dessert requires no *cooking at all!*

PEARS
Red Bartlett

Golden Bartlett

Comice

Anjou

Bosc

GREEN GRAPES

ENGLISH STILTON
Colston Bassett

Tuxford & Tebbutt

Neal's Yard Dairy

ENGLISH PORT
Smith Woodhouse

Dow's Vintage

ENGLISH CRACKERS
Fortt's Original Bath Oliver

Carr's Table Water

A Party for Two

FIRESIDE DINNER

Vegetable Pot Pie

Double Chocolate Pudding

TEN BASIC RECIPES

How many recipes do we *really* need to know? I'm always trying new ideas or writing new recipes in my professional life, but when I'm entertaining I find that I rely on a few old favorites. But how do I keep from serving my friends the same thing every time? The key for me is a core group of good basic recipes that provides a framework for lots of variations.

If you've mastered making a roast chicken with carrots and potatoes, it's a small adjustment to make a roast turkey (page 182) or roast loin of pork (page 244). If you feel comfortable making roasted Brussels sprouts, you can move right on to roasted fennel with Parmesan (*The Barefoot Contessa Cookbook*) or roasted asparagus (page 34). And if you know how to make chicken pot pie, what's so different about making lobster pot pie (*The Barefoot Contessa Cookbook*) or vegetable pot pie (page 255) except a few ingredients? Once I've mastered the process, I find it easy to substitute a few new ingredients.

This applies to dessert, too. I love shortbread cookies (page 210), and I feel absolutely comfortable making linzer cookies and fruit tarts (*The Barefoot Contessa Cookbook*) from the same recipe. If I'm comfortable making pastry cream, adding good dark chocolate and making double chocolate pudding (page 259) is also no stress.

Figure out ten recipes that you love and feel comfortable making. Then write three variations of each one that works for you. Now you've got thirty recipes that are really easy for you to make for a dinner party, and I'd say you're set for a very long time.

VEGETABLE POT PIE
SERVES 4

I love a good chicken pot pie on a cool summer night. For a party it's a one-dish meal that can be prepared well in advance. This new version, with vegetables plus flavorings from Provence, got rave reviews from my friends. The recipe makes enough for four individual pot pies.

12 tablespoons	unsalted butter (1½ sticks)
2 cups	sliced yellow onions (2 onions)
1	fennel bulb, top and core removed, thinly sliced crosswise
½ cup	all-purpose flour
2½ cups	good chicken stock
1 tablespoon	Pernod (see page 222)
	Pinch of saffron threads
1½ teaspoons	kosher salt
½ teaspoon	freshly ground black pepper
3 tablespoons	heavy cream
1½ cups	large-diced potatoes (½ pound)
1½ cups	asparagus tips
1½ cups	peeled, ¾-inch-diced carrots (4 carrots)
1½ cups	peeled, ¾-inch-diced butternut squash
1½ cups	frozen small whole onions (½ pound)
½ cup	minced flat-leaf parsley

FOR THE PASTRY

3 cups	all-purpose flour
1½ teaspoons	kosher salt
1 teaspoon	baking powder
½ cup	vegetable shortening
¼ pound	cold unsalted butter, diced
½ to ⅔ cup	ice water
1 egg	beaten with 1 tablespoon water for egg wash
	Flaked sea salt and cracked black pepper

(recipe continues on next page)

Melt the butter in a large pot over medium heat. Add the onions and fennel and sauté until translucent, 10 to 15 minutes. Add the flour, reduce the heat to low, and cook for 3 more minutes, stirring occasionally. Slowly add the stock, Pernod, saffron, salt, and pepper, and bring to a boil. Simmer for 5 more minutes, stirring occasionally. Add the heavy cream and season to taste. The sauce should be highly seasoned.

Cook the potatoes in boiling salted water for 10 minutes. Lift out with a sieve. Add the asparagus, carrots, and squash to the pot and cook in the boiling water for 5 minutes. Drain well. Add the potatoes, mixed vegetables, onions, and parsley to the sauce and mix well.

For the pastry, mix the flour, salt, and baking powder in the bowl of a food processor fitted with a metal blade. Add the shortening and butter and mix quickly with your fingers until each piece is coated with flour. Pulse 10 times, or until the fat is the size of peas. With the motor running, add the ice water; process only enough to moisten the dough and have it *just* come together. Dump the dough out onto a floured board and knead quickly into a ball. Wrap the dough in plastic and allow it to rest in the refrigerator for 30 minutes.

Preheat the oven to 375 degrees.

Saffron is the stamens of crocuses. The finest saffron comes from Spain and Turkey. Don't use the powdered kind.

Divide the filling equally among 4 ovenproof bowls. Divide the dough into quarters and roll each piece into an 8-inch circle. Brush the outside edges of each bowl with the egg wash, then place the dough on top. Trim the circle to ½ inch larger than the top of the bowl. Crimp the dough to fold over the sides, pressing it to make it stick. Brush the dough with egg wash and make 3 slits in the top. Sprinkle with sea salt and cracked pepper. Place on a baking sheet and bake for 1 hour, or until the top is golden brown and the filling is bubbling hot.

DOUBLE CHOCOLATE PUDDING

Remember My-T-Fine chocolate pudding? It's the ultimate comfort food. Well, I like to take something familiar and bump up the flavor with high-quality ingredients. This pudding gets its flavor from good cocoa powder and imported semisweet chocolate. It's the real thing and, sur-prise!, it's not much harder to make than the packaged kind, and it's sooooo much better.

6	extra-large egg yolks
½ cup	sugar
¼ cup	cornstarch
3 tablespoons	very good cocoa powder
	Pinch of salt
2 cups	milk
1 ounce	very good semisweet chocolate, chopped
2 tablespoons	unsalted butter
1½ teaspoons	pure vanilla extract
2 tablespoons	heavy cream

Beat the egg yolks and sugar until light yellow and thick in the bowl of an electric mixer fitted with the paddle attachment, on medium-high speed. On low speed, add the cornstarch, cocoa powder, and salt. Bring the milk to a boil in a medium saucepan and, with the mixer on low, slowly pour the hot milk into the chocolate mixture. Combine well, then pour the mixture back into the pan.

Cook the mixture over low heat, stirring constantly with a whisk or wooden spoon, until thickened. If the mixture begins to curdle, remove it from the heat and beat it vigorously with a wire whisk. Remove the pan from the heat, add the chocolate, butter, vanilla, and heavy cream, and mix until the chocolate and butter are melted.

Pour into serving bowls. Place plastic wrap directly on the top of the pudding, and chill thoroughly.

CREDITS

Unless otherwise indicated, tableware shown in the photographs is privately owned.

PAGE 1: Flatware from Roots (212-324-3333); olive dish and blue glasses from Broadway Panhandler (212-966-3434); apricot napkins from The Monogram Shop (631-537-3379)

PAGE 11: Plate from Comerford Hennessy at Home (631-537-6200)

PAGE 24: Linens from Nancy Koltes at Home (212-219-2271); flowers from Bridgehampton Florist (631-537-7766)

PAGE 28: Glass pitcher and cake stand from Kinnaman& Ramaekers (631-537-3838); flowers from Bridgehampton Florist

PAGE 42: Flowerpots from Bridgehampton Florist; plate from Lars Bolander Antiques (631-329-3400)

PAGE 54: Candlestick from Nancy Corzine (212-223-8340)

PAGE 59: Plate from Sentimento (212-750-3111); napkin from Tabletop Designs by Stephanie Queller (631-283-1313)

PAGE 67: Bowl from Malmaison (212-288-7569)

PAGE 72: Silver bowl from Tabletop Designs by Stephanie Queller

PAGE 74: Linens from Nancy Koltes

PAGE 87: Linen towel from The Grand Acquisitor (631-324-7272)

PAGE 92: Blanket from Dean & Deluca (212-226-6800)

PAGE 106: See page 1 credit; yellow pitcher from Mecox Gardens (631-287-5015)

PAGE 116: Fork from Roots

PAGE 120: Green chargers from Medox Gardens; green glasses from Campagna Home (212-420-1600); glass vases from Bridgehampton Florist; napkins and flatware from Tabletop Designs by Stephanie Queller

PAGE 139: Platter from Banana Republic (888-906-2800)

PAGE 144: Plate from À La Maison (212-396-1020)

PAGE 168: Silver plates from Hôtel (203-655-4252)

PAGE 173: Silver plates from Hôtel

PAGE 174: Flowers from Bridgehampton Florist; napkins from Grand Acquisitor

PAGE 194: All silver from Hôtel; glass cake stand from Kinnaman&Ramaekers

PAGE 210: Glasses from Tabletop Designs by Stephanie Queller; glass plate from Malmaison

PAGE 212: Tumblers from Nicole Farhi (212-223-8811); linens from Takashimaya (212-350-0100)

PAGE 225: Flatware from Tabletop Designs by Stephanie Queller

PAGE 242: Ceramic dishes from Inside Out (631-329-3600)

INDEX